50 YEARS
OF MIRACLES

and Adventures

Raymond Youdath

D1557343

PublishAmerica
Baltimore

© 2006 by Raymond Youdath.
All rights reserved. No part of this book may be reproduced, stored in a retrieval system or transmitted in any form or by any means without the prior written permission of the publishers, except by a reviewer who may quote brief passages in a review to be printed in a newspaper, magazine or journal.

First printing

At the specific preference of the author, PublishAmerica allowed this work to remain exactly as the author intended, verbatim, without editorial input.

Names have been changed to protect the innocent.

ISBN: 1-4241-2875-7
PUBLISHED BY PUBLISHAMERICA, LLLP
www.publishamerica.com
Baltimore

Printed in the United States of America

This book is dedicated to my deceased parents. Their sacrifices, love and patience made my recovery possible. My brother, Joseph and sister, Muncie taught me the meaning of love, which is giving. To, Helen, my Mighty Mite therapist and friend that brought me to a level of independence I never dreamed possible. And my angel wife, Marilyn, whose gigantic heart engulfed me with undying love for fifty years. Her unselfish love guided me through countless storms. The love of our children, Deborah, David and John and our nine grandchildren made our struggles worth fighting for. I could fill a page with the names of people that helped Marilyn and me countless time, and we are eternally grateful. I also know, that without God, none of the above would have come to pass.

CHAPTER ONE

CATALINA ISLAND

I sat at the old dark pine desk that came with my rented eighth floor apartment. I looked over the cluttered desk, and the old grey Royal typewriter, out the window. I tried to concentrate on the keyboard, but my eyes were drawn like a magnet back to the magnificent view.

It was a rare day for Santa Monica. The Santa Anna winds had temporarily cleared the ever present smog and I could see Catalina Island. I mentally escaped my wheelchair and saw myself walking on the beach at Southern California's play ground. I felt the stares of the beach beauties as they wondered who the new guy was. That wonderful picture reminded me of a few years back, before Polio. I reveled in the memory and feeling of sand pushing between my toes, and the pride in my suntan as I walked my hometown beach on Lake Erie. The sand wasn't as white or water as blue, but it had its share of beach beauties.

Catalina Island
Beach in Ohio 1949

My escape was suddenly interrupted as Jack turned the page of his newspaper and coughed violently, as usual, after a night of drinking and too many cigarettes. I looked with disgust and fear at his two hundred pounds buried deep in the faded brown chair. I could tell he was upset, again. Someone said or did something. His anger and vile mood had increased daily over the last couple months.

I looked back out the window hoping to recapture the good thoughts and feelings I had a moment before, but I could not. I was alone and freighted. So alone it hurt. If only I had someone to confide in, and trust. I stared blankly at the typewriter feeling the three thousand miles between me and home.

I looked up to heaven and pleaded, "Dear God, when and how is this all going to end? And why did You take my father from me? He was only fifty-two and I had much to learn." Tears started running down my cheeks as I pictured us working on the farm together.

"Stop this Ray!" I ordered myself, "you can't let Jack see weakness, no matter what." I made sure his view was blocked by his newspaper and quickly dried my eyes. I looked at the keys of the typewriter and the number's four and two stood out. I then visualized the date 1942, and my mind traveled back to that date on a cold evening in late Fall.

It was nine o'clock and my sister and I were in the barn. She was down stairs loading bags of corn on an escalator and I was upstairs stacking the bags.

I called down to her, "Muncie, slow down, I gotta stack these bags."

"What's a matter Raymond, can't keep up?"

"All you have to do is load 'em. I have to stack 'em and the pile is getting high."

The twenty-five pound bags felt heavier with each trip. We had been working since supper and I was getting tired, but hated to admit it.

"Hey, I'm only eleven and you're sixteen."

"But you were just bragging that you were taller and stronger than me."

Damn, I thought. *Caught again.*

Help was impossible to find because of the war, so my sister and I were Dad's right hand. He graded and bagged the corn during the day and we stacked it after school. Dad was up with the sun and in bed when the sun set. I sat on the edge of the opening in the floor and finally admitted,

"Muncie, hold up a minute. I gotta rest." I figured she would really rib me now, but instead she yelled over the noise of the escalator motor.

"Glad you said that. I was ready to fall over trying to keep you busy."

"Think Dad will get another contract from the government next year to grow seed corn?"

"I don't know. We shipped the last order weeks ago."

"Let's go Ray, we have four bags left and we're done."

We finished, shut off the escalator, threw on our coats, turned off the barn lights and ran through the light snow to the garage. We hung our coats next to our stoker-fed furnace and ran into the kitchen. We were surprised to see Dad setting at the table. He still had on his thick red knitted sleeveless sweater.

Surprised, Muncie asked. "how come you're still up?"

There was a cake on the table with five unlit candles.

Dad smiled at us. "We have something to show you." His weathered and callused hand rested protectively on an envelope.

Mother interrupted. "After we say a prayer for, Joey."

We bowed our heads and prayed for brother, Joeys safe return from the Pacific.

Dad looked at Mother. "Hunce, we've been married more than twenty years. When the country went into a depression, we never noticed it because we were always in a depression."

He turned to us. "If it wasn't for the depression, we wouldn't be here today. Five speculators bought these seventy-five acres in 1927. The 'Crash' in 1929 destroyed their dreams. We bought it for eleven thousand dollars. The 'Crash' gave us a chance in life, and did you know your mother had her teeth pulled without Novocain? That five dollars fed the family for a week." He looked at Mother. "You are one tough Hunky."

Her usual retort was an indignant, "I'm not a Hunky, I am a Hungarian!" But tonight she just smiled.

"Muncie," Dad said, "you work hard as any man I know, and Raymond, you can get the tractor stuck as good as any man I know."

We laughed. Any compliment from Dad, even a left-handed one, warmed us tremendously.

Mother cut in. "Get to it, Joe before we have tears."

Dad reached into his red plaid shirt pocket, next to his corn cob pipe, and retrieved a box of wooden matches. He lit the five candles on the cake, then carefully removed a check from the envelope, placing it proudly on the table. The candles reflected in Mother's beautiful blue eyes and on her silver hair.

"This is a government check for the seed corn. *Five thousand dollars*. We have never seen one check for so much money?"

I can still feel the proudness in our small candle-lit kitchen that cool Fall night.

Several years earlier Dad made a deal with a middle-aged German to put a saw mill in our ten acres of woods. Our end of the deal was enough lumber to build a house and barn. Dad used our horse to snake logs to the huge six-foot saw blade, and I used our Ford tractor in the better areas. We had to finish our house by winter forcing us to use fresh-cut wood. I remember putting oil on nails so I could pound them into the hard beech and oak planks. We spent our first winter nailing wallboards and papering. The next summer the unseasoned wood dried and the walls split. Our second winter was spent patching and re-papering.

Dad opened a sales lot on the highway and business flourished. He was a good grower, but our previous location was on a side road. Now, on a main highway, everyone could see our fields of beautiful Mums, Pansy's and Phlox. For the first time there was money for new equipment and tools.

Across the street was a beautiful estate that sat on forty acres. It consisted of a spectacular twenty one room mansion, four barns, three tenant houses, a machine shop, four greenhouses, an ice house, a hundred foot long chicken house, a hundred-foot long storage shed and a big underground storage cellar. The estate was built in 1900 by a shipbuilder. The second owner raised Draft Horses, until one got loose, ran onto the highway and was struck by an automobile, killing a mother and child. The third and present owner, a widow, was confined to a wheelchair. Her late husband had an elevator installed so she could travel between the first and second floor.

She learned my sister was a cosmetologist and arranged to have her hair done. After a couple months, she asked to see my father. She told him his family entertained her since he bought the acreage across from her. She sat in her wheelchair and watched us build our home and plant the fields. Every day she felt like part of our family as she watched us work, play and grow. She explained that management of her estate was overwhelming and the upkeep of twenty-one rooms was too much for her aging maid. Then she dropped a bombshell. She would like my father to own her farm. Stunned, my father expressed his gratitude but explained he couldn't afford it.

"Nonsense," she said. "You don't need a down payment, nor interest, and you can arrange payments to fit your budget." Dad was speechless. She continued, "go home and talk it over with your wife, and think about it for a couple days."

My father was in a mental fog and almost got hit crossing the road.

My mother said, "No! We have been poor for so long, and we're finally getting our heads above water, and now you want to go deeper in depth, I am afraid."

"Hunce," he pleaded. "As a young boy I walked five miles each way to weed onions on that farm for twenty-five cents a day, and now, God has given us a chance to own it. I must follow my dream."

Again, with very little money my father signed papers.

But! It was not a done deal yet. In the background, her relatives had a secret deal pending with a buyer. When my dad entered the picture, they panicked. The owner knew something was going on and she was determined the farm would go where she wanted it to go. The price she quoted my dad was twenty-five-thousand dollars, lock, stock and barrel. The other buyer immediately offered ten-thousand more. Her answer. "Too late, it's sold."

Her relatives, standing to lose their 'cut', took her to court claiming she was incompetent. The court ruled against the relatives.

World War Two ended and our prayers were answered as brother Joe returned home safely. Homes were being built at an astonishing rate. Evergreens were in demand and our business flourished. On my fifteenth birthday I got my first bicycle and wrist watch.

The next year, Dad bought a new 1947 Cadillac. He preferred driving our '41 Ford pick-up, saying the Caddy was for Mother. From 1942 to 1948 were the happiest days of my life.

The wonderful characters I grew up with.

During and after the war help was scarce. Many "Men of the road" trudged past our farm. Route 20 extended from Portland, Main to Portland, Oregon. They would stop and ask for work. My father was the toughest man I ever knew, and had the softest heart.

First and most dear to me was Joe Benson. Dad and I fixed a room for him in one end of the ice house. From the first day he was, "Ice House Joe." He was a five and a half foot tall and an X-Paratrooper. I spent many nights listening to his war stories. Ice house stayed with us for almost five years. His weekends were usually lost to drinking, but he was dependable all week. He told me if I ever got drafted, he would reenlist with me, and keep me alive. I can still see his crooked smile and hear his throaty voice clearly after forty-five years. A week after I got Polio he packed his few belongings and left. With a smile in my heart I think of him often.

Then there was Jim. A circus roustabout. He stood only five foot six inches tall, and was the strongest person per inch I have ever known. A gentle, likable man with dozens of knife wounds and few teeth. The day he appeared was in our slow season. We didn't need help but Dad told him he could stay in our barn a few days and we would feed him 'till he figured his next move. Dad wanted to tear down an old cow barn and, Jim offered to do it. My dad hesitated, then told him to what you can. Jim was a human machine with a sledge hammer. The roof was off in a day and the side walls of the second floor fell to his repeated blows. The third day I was watching with awe as boards and beams that had stood for fifty years flew in every direction. He looked down at me, smiled his toothless grin and yelled, "watch this last corner post go." But, that last post was holding up the floor he was standing on. He disappeared in a cloud of dust and the side walls collapsed on top of him. I feared he was crushed and dug frantically in the rubble to find him. A large twelve by twelve beam was laying across his back. Luckily he landed in a concrete trough that used to catch cow droppings. I found a long six by six stud and worked one end under the beam. I was able to lift it enough for him to scramble out. Miraculously he wasn't hurt. He said I saved his life and asked if there was anyone I didn't like. He would gladly break their arm or leg for me. "Thanks Joe, I'll keep it in mind."

Another day dad and I were in the pasture fixing our milk cows halter. I looked up and saw a man walking down our dirt road from the highway.

"Dad, I think it's someone looking for a job." He looked up and saw the mans left arm was severed between his hand and elbow.

Dad sighed. "O my, what do I say to him?"

He addressed the man. "Morning, what can I do for you?"

The man stammered. "Morning sir, My name is Jim and-a, I was wondering if I could work for some food and a place to stay for a day or two? I'm a hard worker and can keep up with any man."

I studied Dad's weathered face. His expression didn't give me a clue to what he'd respond. He removed his corn cob pipe from his shirt pocket and twisted it as he thought. Then he said to me.

"Ray, take this man up to the house and have Mother give him something to eat, then take him to the bunk room in the barn." He turned to Jim. "Can you handle a shovel?"

The man answered with a wide smile. "Yes sir! I am missing a hand, but I can handle any tool."

The man turned and started walking toward the house. As I passed Dad, I studied his expressionless face, but when our eyes met I couldn't help but reach out and touch his shoulder. Like a boy caught with his hand in the cookie jar, he quickly put his pipe in his mouth and struck a big wooden match. I look back on that day, and understand why, I have so much love and respect for him. Jim did prove he could outwork any man.

Then there was, Scary Jack. He chose to be called 'Preacher'. He was very muscular and more than six feet tall.

He kept to himself and always dressed in black. He stayed in a room above the chicken barn. Early one Sunday morning, Ice House Joe and I sprayed insecticide on our beds of liners. We finished before the temperature reached 75 degrees. On the way back to the barn, Ice House was walking behind the big power sprayer emptying the last of the spray, and clown that he was, he sprayed the preacher's window. In less than a minute the preacher flew out the door, grabbed Ice House by the throat, lifted him off the ground and pinned him against the building. With a knife at, Joe's throat, the preacher's voice boomed in vile contempt.

"How *dare* you invade the sanctity of holy prayer? You are a *contemptuous* hand of Satan!"

By the time I jumped off the big A.V. tractor and ran around the sprayer, Joe's face was bloodless and the knife was pushing against his throat to the point of penetration. There was terror in Joe's face. My heart pounded from fear. Though I was taller, I was no match for the Preacher, especially in his state of mind. I laid my hand on his shoulder, took a deep breath, and with my heart in my throat said.

"Preacher, Joe didn't mean any disrespect, it was really *my* fault."

He turned his head slowly and his eyes burned into mine. I felt like a raw piece of meat a lion was ready to devour. I think I wet myself when his voice from hell said. "Your fault!"

I felt Joe's and my life hung on my next words.

"Yes, I told him to spray the Ivy growing on the face of the building. I'm very sorry if it disturbed you. I would *never* want to interfere with a man talking to his God."

The glaze over his eyes slowly disappeared and I felt his shoulder muscles relax. He removed the knife and he let Joe slid slowly to the ground.

He folded the knife and slid it into his pocket. As he walked through the door, he left a threat hanging in the air.

"*This* may have been a mistake, but Joe has made remarks I found insulting and blasphemous, and I will not tolerate them in the future."

Joe and I looked at each other for a second, then left quickly. Back in the barn we sat on some bales of burlap. Joe's color returned slowly as he tried to clear his throat. Between coughs he lamented.

"Ray, I've jumped dozens of missions and some with nicety percent causalities. But I was never this scared, I *knew* I was dead. I don't know how you stopped him, but I owe you my life."

The next day Dad gave the preacher a weeks pay and told him he would have to leave. I felt bad, but was glad he left.

My mental escape continued as I stared blankly out my window

Dad bought a rifle for protection. Our sales lot brought in cash over the weekends which we kept in a safe. If I became aware of a robbery, his orders were. "Aim at the robbers head and fire. Never say 'stick em up' to a person with a gun. He could kill your Mother or I. Thank God I never had to, but I was prepared to follow his orders.

We rented eight stalls in our barn to a horse trader. He broke and sold wild horses from the West, one of which was a big stallion called Blackie. After church one beautiful Sunday morning in May, I saddled Blackie and led him out of the barn. The six hundred foot dirt driveway from the barn to the main highway was bordered on one side by greenhouses, and the other side by a five-acre field of beautiful blooming Pansies. I mounted the horse, and since I didn't enjoy cantering, I gave him his head. We were at a full gallop in three strides of his powerful legs. I could taste the fresh spring air as we flew past the dozen huge Elms that lined the drive. I planned on riding around the front between the greenhouses and the sales lot then back to the barn. I drew back on the reins to slow him for the turn, but he continued his wide-open gallop toward the main highway a hundred feet away, and closing fast. I remembered a previous owner's Draft Horse ran onto the highway causing two deaths when their automobile hit the huge animal.

I began to panic. I had to turn him before he ran onto the busy highway! Scared, but determined, I leaned far left in the saddle and pulled his left rein with every ounce of strength I could muster, but he continued at a full gallop! I let go of the right rein and used my right hand to help turn the stubborn, black giant. I pulled his lower jaw so far back his saliva drenched my knee as he reluctantly started to turn.

I heard myself yell. "Turn you stubborn son-of-a-bitch or I'll tear your jaw off!"

With his head pulled sideways he remained at a full gallop. There were several trees in the sales lot and I saw we were on a collision course with the biggest one. I knew we'd never make it to the left of the tree. My only chance was going to the right of the tree. I reversed my position and leaned far right and at the last second, the damn horse went left of the tree, missing it by an inch. The next thing I knew I was on my back on the ground looking up at the Maple tree

15

leaves dancing in circles. Dazed and confused I finally realized I hit the tree with my chest tearing me out of the saddle. I sat up slowly checking my body parts to see what was broken. I stood slowly leaning against the tree trying to get my balance. I half smiled as I realized the horse won and got me off his back, but then I saw the scary picture of what would have happened if my foot had stuck in the stirrup. My blood boiled as I realized he tried to *kill* me. I stumbled to the house and got the 30-30 rifle and on the way to the barn I loaded it with Silver tip bullets. Just then my dad came out of the machine shop. "Where you going?" he asked.

"I'm gonna shoot that fuck'n horse." That was the first time in my seventeen years that I said that word in front of my father.

"Wait a minute, shoot who? And why?"

He grabbed my arm and tried unsuccessfully to stop me.

"Blackie!" I yelled. "He ran me into a tree trying to kill me, and it's a miracle he didn't. He has to die."

"Raymond! It's not our horse and we'll have to pay for him. Besides, he's just a dumb animal."

I stopped, not sure if I could have shot him anyway. Dad took the rifle and told me to put him back in his stall, and then to water the bed of Daphne cuttings. I went into the barn and Blackie was standing by his stall.

"You're lucky this time you big shit."

I yanked off his bridle and saddle then opened his stall gate. He ran directly to his oat bucket. "It'll be a long time before you get any food from me." I then went to water the beds. A half hour later I was walking to the house and was surprised to see Dad walking toward me loading the Winchester.

"Where are you going?" I asked.

"I'm going to shoot that fuck'n horse!"

"Why?" I asked dumbfounded.

"He got out of his stall, and ran circles in the Pansy patch. He destroyed thousands of my beautiful plants."

I couldn't keep from smiling.

"But Dad," I jibbed. "it isn't our horse and if you shoot him we'll have to pay for him. Besides, he is just a dumb animal."

With the rifle over my shoulder we climbed the back stairs and walked into the kitchen. Mom asked what we were laughing at. "Just a joke," Dad answered.

My wonderful daydreaming crashed as Jack yelled to get my attention.

"Hey! Why the hell aren't you typing?" He folded his newspaper and grunted as he lifted his hulk out of the brown chair. I knew the keyboard, but Polio knocked out most of my finger extensor muscles, so I made an excuse that my fingers were tired.

"Tired, bull shit!"

"I'll finish this tomorrow."

"Ya, that's what you always say. You should have mailed in by now."

"I know you're right, but Helen is working my tail off. We're working on getting into bed on a sliding board and I'm doing pretty good."

With that, Jack exploded. "What the fuck are you doing *that* for?" I automatically ducked forward expecting him to slap the back of my head. He kept yelling. "Why is that dumb bitch wasting time on that? She *should* be working on getting you strong enough so you can walk to bed."

"Hey Jack, I'd love to be able to jump into bed, but I gotta face facts. I'll work toward that, but if I can become more independent now."

"More independent! He shouted. "You mean to crawl around like a fucking animal. That's bull shit! I'm not sacrificing my time and effort so you can gimp around on your belly."

"Gee, I thought you'd be pleased. I do pretty good for what muscles I have." Jack stormed back to his chair and dropped onto it so hard I thought it would break. He grabbed the newspaper, tore through it, then jumped up and threw it on the floor

"Common," he demanded. "I'm putting you to bed."

"Now?"

"I don't want to hear about it. I'm going out. Go to bed now, or when I get back."

"Raymond, you dummy. You had to open your big mouth. I guess you're better off going now and maybe he'll cool off by the time he returns."

When Jack became angry, his eyes would glare and his lips would squeeze tight like he was trying to keep something from spilling out. He put me to bed, shut off the lights and slammed the door as he left.

I lay in the dankness and my brain swirled in deep confusion, desperate to find something to cling to. "O God," I prayed. "Will this *ever* end? You're the only one I can turn to." I wrapped the telephone cord around my arm, put the rosary on my stomach and said my prayers ending with. "It's in Your hands Boss, all in, Your hands."

Sleep was impossible. Hours later I heard his key fumbling in the lock. Jack was talking to someone as they came into the room and shut the door quietly.

"Don't worry," Jim whispered. "He's sleeping."

"O No!" I thought. He had told me he made arrangements with a girl at his bar to rape me. It was his way to break my religious wall. I pretended to be asleep as they walked past the foot of our beds. My heart was beating so violently I was sure they heard it. I heard the other person whisper. "Are you sure this is all right?"

"Sure." Jack responded. I was relieved to hear a man's voice, then

I began to worry about him. I peeked out my right eye and saw two figures outlined by the dim light filtering in the window. They got into Jack's bed which was about a foot from mine. My body trembled uncontrollably. Who is this other person? Is he a pickup? Is he a prostitute? Is he one of those men that rob gays? And mostly, what will they do to me? I listened to their moans and groans, then suddenly my fear turned to rage. I wanted to jump up and throw them both out the door. I strained exerting every ounce of strength I had— "God, please help me." I said to myself hoping, but nothing moved!

I had to do-say something. I knew I was in no position to demand anything, but all at once I heard myself saying out loud. "Jack, your life is your business. You can do anything you wish, but please don't bring it here." My heart was in my throat. They were silent for what seemed an eternity, then without a word they got up, dressed and left. My teeth chattered 'til I thought they'd break. I prayed, concentrating on the words over and over until my nerves began settling down. I struggled trying not think about my situation.

Ten minutes later Jack returned. He undressed in the dark, walked to the dresser and picked up something. On his the way to his bed he started talking to himself.

"There's only one answer, this knife."

He always talked about suicides in the gay community, which now worried me about my safety. He deeply resented my association with any girls. He sat on his bed, then lay on his right side with his back to me. "I knew when I bought this knife, it would be special, and it is— my salvation." Then he turned his head and spoke.

"Ray, I'm sorry for any unhappiness I've caused you. I do feel good that I got you to this place and you are improving. Pray for me Raymond, pray that I have the strength *this* time."

"Jack!" I pleaded. "Don't talk like that."

But he kept talking as if in a trance. "One, two, three—Oh, that hurt, but it feels good too—I—finally—did it. The blood feels warm. I thought it would hurt worse, but it really doesn't."

"Jack! For God's sake, don't do this to yourself!"

Ignoring my pleas, he continued rambling. "Oh, the blood is so warm, and, I feel, finally at ease. Remember, Raymond—pray—for—meeee." His voice trailed off and I strained to see him in the darkness as my brain swirled helplessly trying to comprehend the pictures flashing before it. He had moved the phone out of my reach so I couldn't call anyone and no one could hear my voice. When would anyone check on us? Then when they did. The police, the newspapers and poor mother. I could see the headlines. "MAN COMMITS SUICIDE IN PATIENT'S ROOM." Oh boy, oh boy. Then suddenly I heard him move as he rolled on his back Relieved he was still alive I strained to see him in the faint light. I looked for the blood but it was too dark to really see.

"Jack! Jack!" I screamed. "Call the switch board while you still can. Jack!"

Suddenly, he started to snore. The deep and raucous snore of a drunk.

My pity quickly turned to hate.

"You lousy son-of-a-bitch!" I yelled as I realized it was all an act. I looked for something to throw at him. I had to do something, but again I had to accept the fact that I was totally helpless. The Raymond I was for nineteen years, was dead. I would always have to beg someone to exist. How lucky people are that can function on their own. My heart ached as I thought back and saw myself Jump out of bed, hop on one leg as I put on my pants, run down a flight stairs, get breakfast, feed myself and use to the john when I wanted to. Then I saw me kneeling next to my mother and father's bed to kiss them goodnight, every night—. Tears formed as I knew it would never-happen-again.

"Sleep Raymond, sleep. Thinking of what was—what will *never* be again—will drive you crazy. Accept, pray, accept, pray, believe and try to sleep."

But no matter how I tried, my shivering body kept me from sleep.

"Think Raymond!" I demanded. "Think dammit!" My mind searched frantically trying to picture something, anything. I began to panic. Was I losing my only ability to escape?

Then, a picture flashed in my mind, and for an instant I saw a toothy grin and a red crew cut. My mind grasped the picture like a drowning man's death grip on a life ring. I flinched as I saw a dung-covered cow tail swishing toward me, then I saw me on our farm and I was in the field driving our big grey Ford tractor.

It was a steaming day in July and I had one hour before Chuck and Jack would pick me up. I looked over the field of Arborvitae. I already loaded fifty balled evergreens on the trailer and there were a dozen more scattered in the field. I knew I would be late if I drove to the sales lot, unloaded and returned for the rest, so I steered the big tractor into the field trying to avoid the holes left from digging. As I bounced through the field, I looked at my watch.

"You have less than an hour to finish, water the plants and shower. You gotta hustle."

The powerful tractor pulled its heavy load through the field next to the first group. I quickly scanned the roads for my father knowing he wouldn't approve of what I was about to do. He was nowhere in sight so I jumped off leaving the tractor in gear. I ran to the left side and threw two plants on the trailer, then grabbed the steering wheel guiding the tractor to the next group. I ran to the other side, threw on three more and ran back to the steering wheel just as the front wheel hit a hole and the tractor lurched to the right. It took all my strength to straighten the wheel while I ran next to the tractor.

"Raymond, you're taking an awful chance. You get your foot

caught under the big back wheel and you're history. Is it worth the chance just to get to Geneva-on-the-Lake tonight? Hell yes! Just think, hundreds of girls all over the resort." I threw the last group on and drove to the sales lot, unloaded the plants, set up the sprinklers, put the tractor in the barn and ran to the big house and in the basement. I threw my clothes in a pile, showered and ran up eighteen steps to the first floor and sixteen steps to the second floor and into the elevator room.

"Op's, Mom let you move back to the front room yesterday because you're keeping the room clean. You've moved back and forth a half dozen times dummy, when are you going to learn? Well no time to think about that now."

I dressed, shaved, splashed Old Spice all over my body and ran down the thirty-four steps and out the door across the yard to the circle drive and dropped to the curb exhausted. I took a dozen deep breaths then looked at my watch.

"Wow! Three minutes to five." I laid back in the grass under the umbrella of a huge old Maple tree.

"Ray," I heard my dad say.

I stood up and turned to see he had walked up behind me.

"Hi Pops," I said proudly. "I got all the plants hauled up and the sprinklers are soaking them."

"Good," he said, then he followed with, "your brother just called from Cleveland and he won't be home until late, so you have to milk the cow tonight."

His words went through me like a bolt of lightning. Stunned, I said, "Aw-w Dad."

Out of the corner of my eye I saw his hand coming and stepped back just in time. I knew better then to question him, but the situation made me react foolishly.

"Well," I answered, "now that I know you're serious, I'll be glad to milk old Bessie."

With a hint of a smile he answered, "I thought you might."

I turned and ran back to the house and in the basement for my old clothes. I ran up the eighteen steps to the kitchen, got the milk pail, flew down the back steps hitting every fourth one and ran the hundred yards to the barn, then remembered Bessie was out in the pasture.

I dropped the pail and ran to the pasture gate, where she was waiting.

"Thank God I didn't have to look all over the field for you."

I opened the gate and started to lead her to the barn.

"Move faster!" I insisted as I slapped her flank. Her response was to drop a big cow pie. She ambled to her stanchion and I closed it around her neck, then I threw her a fork full of hay and grabbed the milking stool.

"Don't forget to tie her shitty tail," I reminded myself. "You don't need to get slapped with it when she swishes at flies."

I tied her tail to the wall, sat on the stool and forced my left knee into her thigh to keep her from kicking the pail, then grabbed her larger hind teats.

I did enjoy the sounds of strong milk sprays hitting the bottom of an empty milk pail.

"Ping-pang, ping-pang." The pitch changed as the pail started to fill.

"Your udder is hard old girl, you are sure ready to milk." I had about three inches of milk in the bucket when my haste nailed me. Her tail slipped out of my quickly tied knot and she slapped me. Debris fell into the bucket. I jumped up yelling.

"You, dumb son-of-bitch. The one time I'm in a hurry you gotta slap at flies' that aren't even there."

I grabbed the pitch fork. "I feel like shoving this up your ass, but you'd probably just shit all over the place."

I stopped, hung my head and chastised myself.

"Why you yelling at her? You're the dummy that tied the knot."

I retied her tail, washed the pail and started over. My fingers were so long my nails dug into my palms with each squeeze. I ignored the pain and soon the bucket was half full of warm milk, then, "Hey, You-dath! What the hell you doing?"

It was Chuck and Jack. Jack continued. "Is that all you do is play with tits' all day? No wonder you farmers are always smiling, girls only have two."

Jack was the jokester of the two but today I wasn't in the mood. He stood behind me bent over with his hands on his knees. His toothy grin, freckles and red hair gave me a nasty idea.

I said to myself, "Should I or shouldn't I?"

His heckling continued. "Are you getting a hard on squeezing them?"

That answered my question. I leaned back, locked two teat's full of milk with my thumbs and forefingers, aimed and squeezed. Two streams of warm white milk hit him square in the forehead. He straightened up and yelled a string of swear words so loud that Bessie turned her head to see what was happening.

Chuck roared with laughter. "You asked for that one Jack." But Jack didn't see the humor. He stormed out of the barn leaving a blue cloud of swear words echoing between the horse stalls. I looked out the barn window and watched his blue Buick leave a cloud of dust all the way to the main highway.

"Bessie, looks like I'm not going to Geneva tonight." But the sight of the white milk running out of his red crewcut, over his freckles, and into his sputtering mouth made the hectic day well worth it. With a smile on my face, that picture was the last thing I remembered until the alarm went off the next morning.

CHAPTER TWO

DEFIANCE

Jack acted like nothing happened. Anger and frustration stuck in my throat. He knew I couldn't do a thing, and he was right. After he dressed and lifted me to my chair, he went back to bed. I wheeled to the dining room, got my usual order, and began eating.

"Hey Ray, do you eat pancakes every day?"

"What? Oh, hi Augie. Yeah, I guess so."

"Mind if I eat with you?"

"Course not. Sorry, I'm off in a dream world."

A kitchen girl put Augie's tray on the table. "Thanks Gin," Augie said as he leaned his Kenney stick (crutch) against the table, held on with his good hand and dropped onto the chair.

"Glad these chairs are padded," he chuckled, then asked, "did you hear what happened last night?"

Oh crap, I thought. *Who saw what?* I answer casually, "no, what happened?"

"You knew Bill got hand controls on his new Chevy."

I nodded yes.

"He's been driving all over, happier then flies on shit. Well, last night he drove down to Venus to the Aragon Ball Room for the Laurence Welk show. After the show he drove along the coast and parked by the beach for a smoke. A load of punks parked behind him and demanded money. He gave them his wallet and pleaded not to be hurt, explaining about his artificial legs."

"Oh God, Augie, he just graduated from crutches to canes last week."

"Right, and the dirty, rotten, mother fuckers yanked him out of his car, pulled off his artificial legs and beat him with them."

"Is he—?"

"They would have beat him to death but he managed to pull himself under his car. Luckily a carload of college kids stopped and the bastard's drove away."

"How is he?"

"He's at Kaiser with a couple fractured ribs. But worse, they beat open the stub ends on both legs. The doctors hope the damage isn't irreversible."

"Sons-a-bitches. The poor guy gets his legs blown off in Korea fighting for his country and some worthless slime—."

"Damn, you're afraid to go out."

"That settles it Augie, I'm getting a gun. To rob you is one thing, but *they* want to hurt you. I'm not going to suffer through years of rehabilitation to get set back by some degenerates."

"You're right Ray, but it's near impossible to get a permit."

"I'd rather be alive to face that, then be a dead, law abiding citizen."

"I've heard robbers use their victim's guns on them."

"Sure, if you're a fool. It's like owning a car. It's also a lethal weapon, if your stupid. You have to practice till it's second nature. You can't wait until you're in a crises and scared. You must be sure about every function of your weapon and never draw it unless you intend to use it."

"I don't know if I could do that."

"Then don't have a gun. I've handled guns since I was ten and I was taught to respect their awesome power."

"Hell, I'd rather use the gun in my pants, and you're right, the more you practice, the better you get."

"Augie, you ain't old, but you *are* a dirty old man."

"Thanks for the compliment and speaking of horny, here comes that cute new student nurse. "Hi Ann, how about joining us?"

"Sure, if I'm not interrupting. You look like you're in deep conversation."

"Naw, we're just solving the world's problems."

She smiled. "I thought you did that at the Cork."

"Those are domestic problems. Ray is solving over population, just shoot 'em."

"Isn't that a rather permanent solution?"

"Ann, my daddy always told me. Don't do it if you ain't gonna do it right." Augie stood up slowly. "I'm late for P.T., I gotta run, well, limp to class. By the way, the gang is going to the Cork tonight. Ann, talk Ray into coming. He's a stick-in-the-mud."

Augie left and I was embarrassed. How I longed to go and have fun. To laugh and joke and have a few drinks, to hold a girl—. Eight months without any social fun. Eight months of watching others have fun. Eight months of giving excuses, and all because of Jack.

"How about it, Ray. I'll push you over."

"You have a beautiful smile Ann. Your blue eyes light up your face accentuating your chocolate hair. Even with that silly nurse's cap, you are a picture—."

I noticed her puzzled look, and shut up. She stared at me and said. "I've talked to you a dozen times and you barely acknowledged that I was there. I was beginning to think I was invisible."

I was in trouble. I couldn't tell her my true feelings, then slam the door shut.

She continued. "I'm not sure if that was just a line, but it did feel good hearing it. Does that mean okay for tonight?"

I answered automatically. "Wild horses couldn't stop me."

"Great. What else did your daddy advise you?"

"To appreciate beauty."

She smiled. "I'll meet you in the lobby at eight." Then left.

I felt great. I was sure everyone in the cafeteria was looking at the smiling fool. I looked around quickly. Then, as if a barrel of ice water was dumped on me, my smile and soaring spirit—CRASHED!

"What the hell have you done? For eight months you've held back your feelings. A thousand scars on your tongue from biting it, and now— your words come out like an artesian well of shit. How are you going to get out of this? Jack's on a roll from last night and now your going to pour Gaul down his throat. And you're so close to not needing his help. Now you'll blow all the time, money, sweat and pain. What would he do? Would it push him over the brink? Oh God, what do I do?"

A voice interrupted my thoughts, "Ray! Ray! I've been waiting fifteen minutes. You've never been late before. Is something wrong?"

"I'm sorry, Helen. I was deep in thought."

"You don't look too good. Do you want to skip therapy today?"

"No, I'd rather keep busy. Less time to think."

"Ray, let's skip P.T. and go to occupational therapy."

Helen, my wonderful therapist and friend. My 'mighty mite'. She has brought me from helplessness to LIFE. Her boundless knowledge and tenacity are unequaled.

"Any other day I'd make you push yourself, feel honored."

"I do."

"Classes don't start till ten o'clock. We'll have the department to ourselves."

We took the elevator to the mezzanine. She pushed me along the row of silent pulleys, then between the double row of standing bars with an empty harness hanging over each pair. We had to weave through a maze of exercise mats to the back of the department, past sinks, toilets, tubs, showers and then, finally the beds.

"Here we are Ray. Today we'll see if our months of work pays off. You will get into bed by yourself."

"By myself?" I gulped.

"Yes. You tried the sliding board before, but you weren't quite strong enough."

I locked my chair next to a bed and removed the right arm. She continued. "I took your suggestion and sprayed the sliding board with Pledge."

I leaned over and slide one end of the board under my bottom and put the other end on the bed, then tried to move my tall frame across the board without losing my balance.

"I'd be less scared walking a tightrope across Niagara Falls."

"I know you're scared Ray, but remember, I never dropped you in eight months."

I strained every ounce of strength I could muster—and—slid a few inches. Balancing my body at a certain angle let me use my stronger right arm more productively—and I moved several more inches—then, I found myself sitting on the bed.

"Does that smile mean you're proud of yourself, Raymond?"

"You kidding, I'm ecstatic. I never thought I'd—really.—Helen, I—."

"Okay, okay, I know. But before you get too comfortable, what are you going to do now?"

"Now? You mean, *right now?*"

"Yes. *Right now.*"

"A-ah, you pull me back?"

"No."

"I try to slide back?"

"No."

"Then what?" I asked puzzled.

"What do you do when you get into bed? Lay down."

Sweat popped out every pore of my body.

"Lay down! By myself! How do I get my legs into bed? I'm so damn tall it's like dropping a giant Red Wood. I could go off the other side of the bed."

She smiled. "Hold—your—knee—and—rock—back."

"But if my hand slips and I flop back, my feet will stay on the pedals. My adductors are so tight and my legs so long it'll tear the tendons hooked to my spine."

"Raymond, I know you know your anatomy and what does what, but remember, I taught you. Calm down and think. You have figured things out before and you'll also get this. You have a good sense of balance and leverage. Use your head and *think.*"

God, I loved that five-foot hunk of dynamite. She had a way of making me believe in myself.

First I pulled my right leg onto the bed then held my left knee. I looked at Helen, swallowed hard, and said. "Here I go."

I felt like a Bungee Jumper going off a bridge backwards, without the cord. I hit the bed hard, but I still had my knee in my hand and I rolled on my right side. Suddenly the realization hit me. I WAS IN BED, LAYING DOWN, AND I DID IT MYSELF. FOR THE FIRST TIME IN FIVE YEARS. Helen sat on the bed next to me, and we both cried.

A few minutes later, she helped me sit up and I slid back onto my chair.

"We'll get you independent, Ray, and soon."

Authors note: A week later I achieved my second greatest victory. I was able to slide out the back of my wheelchair onto and off a toilet, unassisted. I wrote my mother this note:

Dearest Mother,
TODAY I AM A KING
WITH GOD'S HELP, I RECEIVED MY CORONATION.
I HAVE ASCENDED, UNAIDED, UPON THE THRONE.

Then I remembered Jack and my predicament.

"What's wrong Ray? You were high-as-a-kite a minute ago."

"I—A-a-ah—have—some problems."

"Jack?"

"Yes, but how did you know?"

"I could see the pain in your eyes whenever he was around. I also felt his resentment toward me. He does not want any outside interference with you, and I know what he is."

That hit me like a ton of bricks.

"You—know?"

"Ray, the world has jumped ahead of you in the last five years. When you live in California, his type is easy to pick out."

I felt stupid, and wondered who else knew, and what they thought of me.

"Gee Helen, do you think that I—?"

"Don't be silly. I knew you were in trouble. That's why I've been pushing you so hard to be independent. If you want to talk about it, I'm here. Seriously, I don't know how you've kept it in all these months."

"I've been afraid to tell anyone, and I especially don't know what to do tonight."

I told her about the previous night.

"Are you afraid of him?" She asked concerned.

"When he's drinking, yes."

"If you want to talk, you have my trust."

I felt like a dam ready to burst and couldn't hold back any longer. I explained how I met Jack. How his words of encouragement were the first I'd heard in years. About Mother renting a home in Florida, and that she, Jack, and I went down for the winter. And he did take a tremendous burden off my mother. She returned home a month before Jack and me.

I felt comfortable talking to Helen. I told her I bought a fishing pole and was casting across our quiet street when a girl rode by on a bicycle."

"Any luck?" She joked.

"No, but since you stopped, I'd say I'm having a good day."

She smiled. "My name is Judy. I'm staying with my grandparents."

"I'm Ray, it's a pleasure to catch, I mean, meet you."

"That's a fair line, for a guy fishing on a street. You're new here, did you buy?"

"Just renting till April. Where do you live?"

"Lauderdale By-The-Sea. I'm a student nurse and assigned to Holy Cross around the corner and I'm heading to work now. Will you be fishing tomorrow about noon?"

"Absolutely."

"Good, see you then."

I watched her ride away, and smiled to myself. "It's been a while Raymond, but you still got it."

We met the next day and talked a long time. Jack told me to invite her to lunch and she accepted. The next day after lunch, Jack said he was going to see a movie and would be back in a couple hours.

"He's a nice guy," she said.

She sat on my lap, we kissed and talked for two hours. It did a lot for my wounded ego. Soon we realized three hours had passed and she left to go to work. Two hours later, Jack came home with a bottle of whiskey. He was drunk and kept drinking. When he went to the bathroom, I emptied the whiskey bottle into the kitchen sink. He was livid, and smashed the empty bottle in the sink, and kept yelling. "Life ain't fucking worth living, and you gotta deny me a drink, you selfish prick." I hid his car keys before he stumbled out to buy more whisky. While he was outside, I removed the cylinder pin from my old Colt revolver, and hid it. When he returned, he was worse and screaming more about death. He did get the gun as I feared and attempted to load it, but the cylinder kept falling out. He knew I did something but couldn't figure out what. After two hours of seething he seemed to calm down. I figured I better go to bed before he passed out, but when he put me to bed, I found the reason for his actions. He was gay and he raped me. I hit him as hard as I could, but my strength was inadequate. The next day he cried and apologized, blaming it on whiskey. I called home and told my brother. His answer was not to worry about it. I was devastated and confused by his reply, but finally realized the sad truth. I was alone, helpless and twelve hundred miles from home. What could I do? My sister had three children. I'd already half killed my mother, so I never fished in the street again. I knew that was his plan, but I had no choice. From then on I slept with a rosary on my stomach.

He would occasionally jibe acidly. "You think that fucking thing can protect you?" As long as he was sober, it did.

A month later, without further incident, we returned to Ohio. The kind Industrialist was happy with my progress and offered to send Jack with me to a rehabilitation center in California. I knew it was my one chance in life, and as long as Jack was sober, I should be all right. I prayed I was making the right decision, and because of you Helen, I did."

"How you kept it all inside and kept smiling, I'll never know. We'll work twice as hard."

"Thanks, I truly owe you my life. I was invited to go out tonight and dammit, I *am* going. He is *not* going to run my life any more."

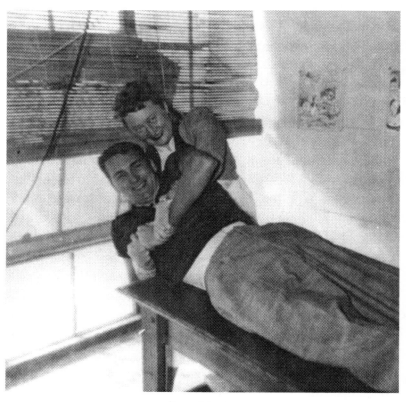

Santa Monica
My "Mighty Mite" Therapist

I could hardly eat supper worrying how I would tell Jack I was going out. Back in our room I wheeled by the phone a dozen times to cancel my date. Finally, with my heart in my throat, I blurted out, "Jack, I'm going to the Cork with the gang tonight. Do you want to come along?"

He kept the newspaper in front of him. I repeated the question. Still no response, so I left the room.

As I wheeled to the elevator, I chastised myself. "Are you stupid or what? Why the hell did you ask him to come. Think that'll make things better? Being thoughtful never did any good before. Sometimes I wonder about you, Raymond."

The elevator doors opened. "Hi Arnie, how's it going?"

Arnie, an Oriental always had a wide friendly smile. "You know, my day up and down. Six floor, Ray?"

"No movie tonight Arnie, going next door with the gang."

I wheeled into the lobby and Ann was at the reception desk. "Hi, am I late?"

"No, I had some letters to post. Ready to go?"

"Sure, but I must say. You look great in street clothes."

"You miss my hat."

We laughed as she pushed me out the front door and down the sidewalk to the Boardwalk that extended from the Santa Monica Pier to Venus and, Lawrence Welk's Aragon Ball Room. We turned north toward the Pier. It was a beautiful starry night and the roar of the waves were like music.

"I love Santa Monica," she said. "Hope I can R.N. near the ocean somewhere."

"This is sure better than the snow and cold in Ohio. The white stuff is pretty, but only to look at."

With, Jack on my mind, small talk was difficult. What was he doing? How would he be when I got home? Would he even *be* there? I had a bad feeling.

The lounge was directly across from Muscle Beach. The weights, stands and bars the body builders used looked eerie as they reflected the lights from the long, high, Santa Monica Pier.

"Ever come here in the daytime and watch the 'muscle men' work out?" I asked.

"It is a sight. All the girls are ow-o-in and aw-in over the tanned muscular bodies, and the 'muscle men' are ow-o-in and aw-in over each other."

"You got that right." I laughed.

A 'Jam Session' was playing as we entered the club. A group of Beach People were enjoying the local talent. Our gang was on the opposite side of the room. The music was mellow and 'trendy'. Augie waved at us. I was surprised to see a couple therapists and several patients.

"Hey, Ann, how did you get, Ray out?"

"We vamps have our ways."

"This is the first time I've seen you here," one of the P.T.'s commented.

Several others chimed in with the same comments, making me uneasy.

I covered. "You're right. I have lots of drinking to catch up on."

I sat back quietly until the third round when a warm wave began to relax me. I hadn't had that feeling in for a long, long time. I actually forgot about Jack, and Polio.

Each person made a toast. When it was my turn, I held up my glass. "My toast is short. Here's to honor—Get on 'er and stay on 'er."

Their laughs were fuel to my long, idle self. I found myself dominating the table with jokes and comments.

Everyone left around ten o'clock. We laughed and sang all the way back to the institute. Ann and I went through the Spanish Archway to the institutes walled patio on the beach. There were a dozen lounges, chairs and tables. Part of the group stopped to talk and have some smokes. Ann sat on my lap and we shared a cigarette.

"This was a great night," I said. "It's been a long time."

"Where did you get all those stories? My jaw still aches."

"Really? My mother always said a kiss makes everything feel better."

"I'm getting to like your family, a lot."

"Wait till I get to what my sister told me."

"I can hardly wait."

Her kisses brought back warm memories. After a couple cigarettes, we went inside.

We got on the elevator and Arnie smiled. "Going home, kids?"

Home! And Jack! The thought ripped through my stomach and slapped me back to reality. I got so deep in thought, I didn't realize the elevator door was open.

Ann jibed, "hey, party boy. Wake up."

The eighth floor was U-shaped. My room was on one end of the U and the nurse's quarters were on the other end. She kissed me on the cheek and we parted. The ten-yard trip to my door seemed endless. Every turn of my wheels put a different picture in my mind, and they were all bad. I sat outside my door for ten minutes before I turned the doorknob. The light was on in the sitting room. I wheeled through the dark bedroom and found the sitting room empty. I went back to check the beds. No Jack. I didn't know whether to feel relieved or more worried. I went into the sitting room and tried to read or write. I couldn't concentrate on either. At midnight I went into the bedroom and pulled the phone onto the bed. I thought of calling, Helen or Robert. I met Rob a couple weeks earlier at the pool where he worked helping patients. He was six-seven and we immediately felt a camaraderie because of our similar heights. We become good friends. He told me to call him if I ever needed anything. As I picked up the phone, I heard a fumbling with the lock. I heard Jack swear as he pushed the door open. It slammed against the wall and he swaggered as he stepped in. I flinched as he slammed the door shut. The sound echoed through the room and down the hall. He glared down at me through bloodshot eyes. His huge frame loomed menacingly above me, and his foul whisky breath poured over me. He stabilized himself with his fat hand on the wall. God, how I hated the smell of alcohol. "I've been drinking, so what!" His face contorted from drink and anger. "It's none of your, God damn business, what I do on *my* time."

"You're right, Jack, it's none of my business. Just come into the sitting room—."

He stopped my chair from turning with his foot. "Don't gimmy that bull shit! You just want me to sit down and fall asleep."

"No," I pleaded. "Really, I just want to talk."

His balance worsened, and his stammering increased, as he became more vile.

"I'm sick of talking. I'm tired, and I want to go to bed. Get that God damn wheelchair next to the bed so I can finish my *duties*."

"Oh God," I pleaded. "Cure me for just ten minutes. Restore my body to what it was before I got Polio." I pictured my six-six frame, and what I'd do to this drunken fat bastard. But, realizing it was a hopeless dream, I continued to plead. "Jack, after we talk—."

He cut in yelling. "What's a matter? Afraid I'll see you naked? Who the hell do you think you are? You and yer fucking high and mighty family. You all *think* yer, God's gift to the world."

I'd heard the rhetoric many times, but the violence in his voice scared me. I knew I wasn't safe going to bed now. He started pushing my wheelchair toward the bed. I knew I had to stop him, so I locked my brakes.

"God dammit!" He screamed at the top of his lungs, with saliva spitting out of his mouth. "You ain't getting away with it this time, you spoiled prick!"

Without warning, his giant right hand came off the wall and smashed against the left side of my face. The powerful blow sent my upper body over the right arm of my wheelchair. I felt my bottom lift off the cushion. Luckily my right hand hit the bed, keeping me from falling out. I rocked back onto my chair. I heard vertebrae snapping throughout my spine. The shock took my breath away and I felt very dizzy. I had faced this situation countless times and I had always convinced him to sit down and talk, until he would pass out. I'd wait several hours, until three or four in the morning, then wake him. He would then be meek and begging for forgiveness, always blaming the alcohol, but this was the first time he reverted to violence.

Suddenly, he picked me up and stumbled between the beds and dresser toward the window. My feet dragged across the dresser, scattering everything. He began babbling. "If I can't have you, nobody will."

Then, in a melancholy voice, said, "all you had to do was let me have you—hell—once a month. At least I would have something to look forward to."

Then his rage returned. "But no! You and your fucking Rosary on your stomach—what good is, He doing you now? Well, since, He won't make you walk, maybe, He'll make you fly." He lunged forward. I felt our bodies crash through the window and we were in the air mingling with broken glass and screen. We fell in a slow, twisting motion. I saw the concrete boardwalk coming up to meet us. I wondered why I felt no pain. I heard laughter and saw the glow of cigarettes on our patio from patients enjoying the Santa Monica night. I saw waves crashing on the beach and the foam was shining bright, in total blackness. I remembered being told it was the phosphorous in the salt water. Then, fear overwhelmed me, as I realized death was inevitable and pain exploded in my back and neck. Then, absolute silence.

"Where am I?" I wondered. I felt like I was stumbling through a deep fog. "Am I dead?"

Then, in the distance I heard a familiar sound. Afraid of what I would see, I reluctantly opened my eyes slowly. As they focused, I saw two feet on the floor protruding from the end of my bed.

"Jack?" I questioned, trying to clear my head.

The sound, I realized, was the snoring of a drunk. A pain shot down my neck and spine as I turned to look at the window. I was surprised to see the window still intact. I turned my head back slowly, to avoid more pain. I tried to shake the cobwebs from my aching head.

Oh-o Ray, I thought. *Is this how it ends?*

I tried moving parts of my body. Though painful, they moved.

I finally realized we both passed out after he hit me. I looked at my watch.

"It's four a.m., Raymond, and you have eight hours of classes starting at eight. Think you'll make it with a couple hours sleep? You've done it dozens of times before, but this time it's more than just loss of sleep."

I wheeled toward his feet. The three-foot trip was painful, but running into his foot was gratifying. It took a dozen bumps before he struggled to crawl up and sit on the bed. With his elbows on his knees, he buried his face in his hands, and wept.

"Oh God, Ray. Not again! Why do I keep hurting the one person that is so good to me?"

Then he bolted upright, and slowly turned his head. Seeing my red swollen face, he cried out. "I HIT YOU! MY GOD, I REALLY HIT YOU!" He turned his hand palm up and condemned it. "YOU, SON-OF-A-BITCH!" He extended it out and above his eye level and resolved. "YOU ROTTEN, FUCKING HAND! YOU DON'T

DESERVE TO BE THERE!—I'LL CHOP YOU OFF!"

His head dropped into his left hand, and he sobbed, while his right hand hung shamefully in the air.

I let him cry until I was sure he was sober. Swallowing my anger and pride once again, was like drinking Gaul. But again, I had to be practical. "Jack! It's over now, let's go to bed. I have to be in the tub room in a couple hours."

He responded quickly. "Okay, Ray, I'll get you right to bed."

I removed my shirt, shoes and corset. He pulled the covers back, put my feet on the bed, and lifted me onto the welcoming mattress. He laid me back, covered me, reached under the covers and pulled off my trousers. He propped my feet against the footboard. I tried not to react to the pain, but he saw me flinch.

"I'm so sorry Ray. You have so much hurt, and I have to add more. I swear to, God above. I'll never drink again. You'll see, everything will be fine."

He jumped in his bed and within a minute was snoring.

I lay on my back, feet against the footboard and hands crossed on my chest. The exact position I'd slept in for almost five years. Never on my right side, never on my left. Tears welled up in my eyes.

"Oh, Raymond. *What* are you going to do? What *can* you do? Your choices are not that great. If you tell anyone, they'll call the police and he'll be gone. It's the same old problem. What do you do then? You need care, twenty-four hours a day. You're lucky Mother has enough money to pay the bills here. Jack's salary is half paid by his humanitarian employer and you're still dependent. Dressing yourself, using the john, getting in or out bed, and—." Dejection overwhelmed me. "You've been here six months and are starting to show improvement. You *can't* go home yet. You've half-killed Mother already by lifting your damn long body. God, why did you make me so tall? You knew Polio was going to happen. If I were a foot shorter, life for everyone would be much, much easier." Frustration and despair deepened. I had to escape this melancholia before it consumed me.

So I attacked myself.

"What the hell are you bitching about Raymond? Forget so soon? Remember going through the ward yesterday? Remember the babies and young children with their twisted and still bodies. You are Superman compared to them. So many of them will *never* hold a glass, *never* feed themselves, and yet, they returned a smile when you passed. Remember the redheaded mother, sobbing into the pillow, on her son's bed. She held his pillow for hours after he died, and *your* complaining? You should be ashamed of yourself."

Clutching my Rosary, I finally fell asleep. My dreams took me back to 1950.

CHAPTER THREE

THE BEGINNING

It was an unusually warm, early spring day. The windows were down on my new 1950 Ford convertible. Rosemary Clooney sang for the seagulls and me as I cruised along the Lake Erie Shore—way into Cleveland. It was April the fourth and my nineteenth birthday was the next day. Despite the nagging pain in my neck I felt on top of the world. "What more could anyone want?" I asked myself.

My polished chartreuse car reflected with pride the morning sun.

"Raymond, in a couple months Geneva-On-The-Lake will open. Hundreds of girls from Ohio and surrounding states will be vacationing there. A new crop of beauties every week, all summer. WOW!"

I smiled as I thought back three days. My family owned an evergreen nursery and I made a delivery to Sears in Cleveland. When I took the bill into the office, I walked past a dozen secretaries. The smiles, and several phone numbers I got, made me feel I was finally becoming a man.

My happy thoughts were interrupted as I drove into the parking lot of City Hospital about ten-thirty. I locked my car, patted the top. "See you soon, me beauty." Little did I know what fate had in store for me.

My mother was waiting at the front entrance. The sadness in her beautiful blue eyes tore at my heart. We embraced and I tried to find words to comfort her. My father, at fifty-two, was killed in an automobile accident two years earlier. My sister and Pete, her doctor husband, were home on leave from Waco Air Force Base in Texas. She became ill and had been in the hospital for two weeks with some strange thing called Polio.

"How's Muncie?" I asked.

"She—seems—okay. She's in isolation."

"What's that?"

"Anyone that goes into her room must wear a mask and gown."

"How long will that last?"

"A couple more days."

"I don't know why they want me to see her doctor, I feel great."

"Pete told Muncie's doctors you weren't feeling well, and since she was here—." We walked up the steps into the hospital. She continued, "are you sure you're okay, Ray?"

My head and back felt lousy for over a week, but I sure didn't want to add to her heartache.

"I'm sure, but since we have a doctor in the family I guess we should humor him. Besides, it gave me a chance to get out of my chores and drive my new car."

"How many times did you wash it last week?"

"Seven, and a wax job."

She laughed and I felt happy at that. My brother-in-law and the doctor were waiting at the desk.

We exchanged formalities and the doctor commented, "They sure grow them tall in the country. How tall are you?"

"Six-six. I know. You didn't think they stacked it that high."

That line always got a laugh, and it did again.

The doctor explained that a spinal tap would verify everything was all right. I was taken to an examining room where a nurse started to hand me a gown. She did a double take at my height. I expected the usual question, but instead she said, "I hope this gown covers everything."

I felt my face flush.

"My goodness, a nice looking young man that blushes. That's a rarity."

I was feeling good with my experiences in the "Big City," until she returned with a young intern with a very big needle. He smiled, "I'll give you a shot with this little one first then all you'll feel is a little pressure. Lay on the table on your side and curl up in a ball"

He was right. They quickly left with my spinal fluid. A half hour later the doctor returned. "The test turned out okay, Ray, but we decided to admit you for a few days of observation."

I found out much later that he lied. My fluid was full of Polio Virus.

"Sure," I answered. "A few days vacation would be fine."

Two orderlies were going to lift me onto a Gurney, but I declined their help and jumped on.

It was a long ride through the bowels of the hospital to a tunnel leading to the contagion building next door. We took an elevator to the second floor then down a long hallway to a room. We were followed in by two nurses with masks and gowns. They were going to help lift me to the bed, but again I declined their help and jumped onto the bed.

One of the nurses asked the orderlies. "Are you sure you brought him to the right place?"

"Yes, but he doesn't look like he needs to be here."

Another nurse entered with a large metal container. "I have a 3-H enema for, Ray Youdath."

"Sorry to say that's me, but what's a 3-H enema?"

They all laughed and one answered. "High, Hot and a Hell-of-a-lot." They were right on all three H's.

"Where's the bathroom?" I asked.

"Afraid not, Doctor ordered that you use the bed pan."

They left the room and I pulled a chair next to the bed. I sat on the pan resting my feet on a chair. I was feeling proud of my ingenuity when suddenly I fell over on my right side. I thought I just lost my balance and pushed myself back up with my arms. I didn't realize it then, but the virus was beginning its killing spree on the motor nerves that moved my muscles.

The rest of the day and evening were like living in a fog. I remember laying in bed without a thought of why I wasn't moving. I can remember thinking. "Soon as I'm out of isolation the nurses don't have to wear masks, boy, we'll have all night to socialize. What stories I'll have to tell my buddies."

That evening my mother was sitting next to my bed when the doctor entered the room. He put his hand on my still arm. "Ray, I don't want you to worry, but you are struggling to breathe."

"I am? I feel okay."

"I know, but you'll be able to sleep easier tonight if we put you in a respirator."

Knowing my mother was listening, I answered, "sure Doc, whatever you think is best."

An iron lung was wheeled into my room. I was so tall the footboard had to be sawed in half and spread apart so the bellows could fit between my feet. The end of the long yellow tube unbolted and the front of the machine rolled out with a long narrow mattress. I didn't jump over this time. It took four people to lift me.

They laid me on the mattress and slid me up until my head went through an opening and rested on a ledge. Then the whole thing rolled together and the four big levers clamped it shut. A nurse put my head on a pillow, and again I didn't wonder why I couldn't lift my head. The fog was getting deeper. She wrapped a cloth collar around my neck to make the tank airtight. Then, with a click of a switch the giant bellows came to life. They pushed air into the tank forcing air out of my lungs. With a whoosh, the out-stroke caused a negative pressure in the tank causing my lungs to expand, drawing air into them. I soon learned the only time I could talk was on the in-stroke.

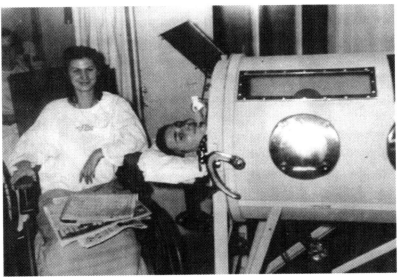

June 1950 Ray's sister Muncie sitting next to him
Then, the longest night of my life began.

The end of my new home was rolled into the hall so I could see the nurses' station in the tilted mirror above my head. There was activity until the eleven o'clock shift change. After that, oh God, the seconds were like hours. The hands on the clock above the nurses' station seemed to never move.

This was the first night I could remember that I didn't say my night prayers on my knees. I shut my eyes and spoke to, Him. "Well, Boss, I can't get down tonight, but I will tomorrow night." I said my regular prayers ending with my usual, "Bless my mother, father, sister and brother. Friends, relatives and enemies. Amen." Usually after that, it was morning, but not this time.

When I looked, my nemesis the clock, moved but a few minutes. I started counting the whooshes per minute, about nineteen. "Okay, that's more than a thousand an hour. Let's see, it's two A.M., That means six thousand whooshes until the morning shift change. I'll surely be glad when tomorrow comes and the doctor gives me a shot or a pill to start my recovery. Well, in the meantime I might as well start count—."

My attention was suddenly drawn to a loud crash. The entrance doors at the end of the hall burst open and several people ran toward me pushing a Gurney. One person was squeezing a thing that looked like the bladder out of a football. A tube ran from it to a girl's throat. The rattle of the wheels echoed off the walls as they spun faster than they were designed to. I felt the breeze as they rushed past me down the hall and into a room. Several nurses ran in behind them. I heard panic in the voices from the room. The only words I could discern were, "Stat! Stat! Stat!" Over and over again. Ten minutes later as the nurses walked out of the room I could hear their muffled sobs. They were followed by the EMS crew pushing the Gurney. The doctor walked next to them with his head down and eyes closed. His hand rested on the Gurney as it guided him down the hall.

As they passed, I saw the outline of her still body under the sheet. The wheels now turned silently giving respect to their charge. I stared at the door long after they exited. For the very first time in my life, doubt crept into that very sacred, private place that always excluded my mortality. Death or serious problems were never for me, but now doubt began to creep in.

"Raymond, that girl was your age, and now she'll never experience another thing on this earth—for eternity. For, e-t-e-r-n-i-t-y!"

My mind was overwhelmed trying to comprehend, *Eternity-no end.* Then another painful revelation.

"Raymond, do you realize what would have happened if you had been home alone tonight? Oh My God! You might not be going home as soon as you thought."

But my optimistic mind prevailed again. "Maybe you'll be here more than a few days, a week or two at the most. After this night ends and some medicine, you *will* be polishing your beautiful convertible under that giant maple tree again."

I struggled to keep that picture in my mind. I struggled to feel the polishing rag in my hand and pouring Duco # 7 on the hood, but the rattling wheels and the outline of the white sheet kept exploding into my mind's picture. I felt tears running down my cheek. As a nurse walked by our eyes met. She wiped my tears, then left without saying a word. With the white outline in my mind I said the Rosary ending with, "Eternal rest grant onto her O' Lord, and let the perpetual light shine upon her. May her soul, and the souls of all the faithful departed, rest in peace, Amen."

Six thousand whooshes later the hallway came to life. I hadn't slept at all. The grandest sight of my life was to see my mother walking toward me. She kissed my forehead and spoke through her mask. "How was your night?"

"It was—okay, how—was yours?"

"I surprised a few doctors when they found me sleeping in their lounge."

She got my breakfast tray. "It's been a long time since I've fed you Raymond, now remember what the doctors said, swallow on the expiration."

I nodded and sucked a mouthful of orange juice through a straw, waited until the whoosh, then swallowed. It tasted wonderful. I finished the O J and the oatmeal. I was doing well, swallowing in rhythm with the bellows. Then came dessert, coconut pudding. On my very first swallow, something stuck in my throat. I tried to cough, but the machine made me inhale at the wrong time. I started choking. I heard my mother screaming for help—Then, oblivion.

Several weeks of horrible nightmares began:

I was laying on a hard granite table with my arms and legs strapped down. A steel cage stood silent guard around me. The room was large with cold green tiles on the floor, walls and ceiling. The only object on the wall was a clock. It's hands never moved. A section of the wall slowly creaked opened. Two student nurses and an R.N. walked up to the cage door. The R.N. unlocked the giant padlock and they entered. I was consumed with a torturous thirst. The dryness in my throat and mouth made words difficult.

"I—glad—you—here. Wa'er—pease—sooo—dry."

The R.N. told a nurse to wipe my lips with a wet wash clothe. The coolness was refreshing, but I needed more, much more. I was so dry I ached. The R.N. sent the two students to get something. As soon as they left she said in a cold voice. "You don't remember me, do you?" She rubbed her hands over my face and chest, then kissed me.

"I—sorry—don't—remember, but pease—I—sooo—dry."

Her voice dripped with venom. "*Good*, I want to see you suffer. I'll enjoy every minute until you *die*." She dangled the damp cloth just out of my reach. When the students returned I begged them for some water, but the RN stopped them. With a sinister smile she discharged them. "Don't worry girls, I'll take good care of him, he can't have too much at a time." I panicked and tried to tell the students not to leave, but they did and we were alone. She tantalized me by dragging the damp cloth across my lips. I grabbed it with my teeth trying to get an extra drop before she could pull it away.

*NOTE: I found out later that I developed pneumonia while in the coma. Nurses would rub ice and a damp cloth on my lips, and I would keep trying to bite it.

Then, I was jarred out of my dream by Jack's booming voice. "Shut that damn alarm off!"

It took a while for me to shake the vengeful nurse out of my head. I started to reach for the alarm and pain shot down my back reminding me what had happened the night before.

Jack finally got up, stumbled past my bed and snarled, "I don't want to hear any crap today. My head feels like it's going to explode."

I felt like saying, "You think your head hurts, wait until you cut off your hand."

His remorseful words from the night before vanished with the morning sun. As he set me up, I gritted my teeth to steel myself from the pain. I was glad when I got to the tank room and, Robert lifted me into the wonderful soothing hot water. I closed my eyes and wondered if the answer, was to slip my head under the water, and end everything.

Margaret, the wonderful lady in charge of the tank room, asked why I was so quiet.

"I must have pulled a muscle in the pulley room."

"Okay Ray. You just rest yourself. The warm water will help."

She was always kind and treated me like a son. We had eaten at her home several times. She called my next class and I stayed an extra half hour.

The next few weeks passed with very little conversation with Jack. Helen and I worked feverishly everyday. I skipped half of my other classes so we could spend more time together. Jack stayed in every night playing the martyr, until one Saturday, he went out after supper.

"I'll be back by nine," he said as he walked out the door.

By two o'clock in the morning I realized something was very wrong. He was never out past midnight. I had no choice but to call Robert. Luckily he was home, and I explained my dilemma. He said he would stop before work to see if Jack returned. He did not. I arranged for him to help me sit up each morning. I would dress myself and wait for him to help me sit up. I did the rest.

Several days after Jack's disappearance, a patient asked if I had heard from him. When I answered "No," he handed me a clipping from the local newspaper. The title read:

"Two Arrested in OP For Morals Offense." It went on to read.

"Two men arrested in a car parked near Bicknell St. and Ocean Ave. They were accused today by police of a felony moral's offense. Booked late yesterday were xxxxxxxxxxxxxx, a sailor and Jack Arthur xxxxxxxx, 39, 1815 Ocean Front."

Dumbstruck, I muttered, "thanks Bob, I—didn't—know."

I rolled to the cafeteria, got a cup of coffee and sat at one of the tables trying to collect my thoughts.

After his third try, I finally heard Augie asking if he could talk to me, I answered yes.

"I see you have a copy of the article about, Jack."

"Yes, I just got it from Bob, did you know?"

"We all did days ago, but didn't know what to say."

"Damn, I don't know what to say or think."

"Can I be honest with you?"

Puzzled, I answered, "sure."

52

"The night you came to the Cork, you surprised the hell out of everyone."

"I did?"

"And how. We all thought you were a spoiled, rich tyrant."

"Me! Why?"

"You never went out with the gang, and whenever, Jack showed up at the bar, he would always comment. "*My keeper let me out tonight.*" He told everyone you resented him going out and that you wanted him to be on the job, at your beckoning, every minute. You turned down all requests to party and you never dated. Consequently, we believed his stories. Then at the Cork the other night, you were exactly the opposite of what we expected. You were a lot of fun. We had even wondered if, you were, you know."

"Oh Jesus. I wondered why some people would shy away from me." I told, Augie the facts.

"Wow! He set you up, and we swallowed his stories, like a bunch of yokels. Boy, I feel like a jerk for the shit I thought. Have you heard from him?"

"Not a word. I was beginning to think he jumped off the pier."

"Too bad the son-of-a-bitch didn't."

"I don't know about that, Augie."

"You mean, after all he's put you through, you can have compassion for him? Hell, if it was me, I'd a helped the bastard jump."

"Sure, many times I felt hatred. But I've known him for a couple years. Outside of his 'quirk' he is an intelligent, caring human being. You may think I'm nuts, but I believe through a mess-up in genes *they* are born with those feelings. Given the option, I'm sure they would choose not to be gay."

"I don't know about that. You've seen *them* on their beach down the boardwalk. Hundreds of them from preteens to old geezers. If they see you look at them, they'll kiss and rub each other in defiance.

Hell, I've heard them say they are proud of what they are."

"What else can they say? Do you tell people you feel different because you walk with a limp and a withered arm at your side? Am I to apologize for being in a wheelchair?"

Augie shook his head. "Christ, Ray, we didn't *ask* for polio."

"My point exactly. Did they ask to be gay?"

"Damn, you get me confused. Then you think what, Jack did to you is excusable?"

"Hell no! That's two different things. He can't help what he is, but he is responsible for his actions."

"This deep stuff hurts my head. I'd rather talk about girls. You and Ann seem to hit it off. Aren't you glad I pushed you together?"

"For that Augie, I'll be eternally grateful."

"I got passes for the arena tonight. Lord Layton, Gorgeous George, Bo-Bo Brazil and a big wrestling card are scheduled."

"You mean the arena up the hill on Ocean Avenue?"

"Yeah, and it's even on TV. Why don't you ask, Ann?"

"Okay, cupid, I—"

"You're in luck. Here she comes now. Well I gotta go to class."

She said yes, and a half dozen patients and pushers met in the lobby. We made our trek up the hill one block to the arena. It was my *first* time out without worrying. We sat in an area for wheelchairs and I enjoyed the show, and my ticket won the jackpot drawing. Ann pushed me to the announcer's table next to the ring. I got a standing ovation from the audience. I was embarrassed, but pleased.

Then, near the end of the fights, a lady in her forties approached me. She was an attractive brunette, and well dressed. She asked if she could speak to me. Puzzled, I answered, "sure."

"I've been watching you all evening. You have the warmest smile I've ever seen. Would you mind if I kissed you?"

"A-a, of course not," I answered.

She leaned down and kissed me on the cheek. She smiled warmly and held my hand. It seemed like we were the only two people in the arena.

"My name is Mary, and tonight, you saved my life."

She turned and melted into the crowd.

Her face and words burned a permanent spot in my mind.

The next day, Sunday, I mailed my winnings to St. Mary's Church in Santa Monica.

Two weeks after, Jack's arrest, I received a letter from him.

Ray, I just talked to my attorney and he told me my bond will be reduced to $500 at the preliminary. I am hoping to be with you next Thursday. Pray for me and if I need help please don't let me down. Regards Jack.

The same day I received a second letter.

Dear Ray. I have been waiting hopefully to be out on bail by now and that is why I have not written sooner. It took a long time for my hopes to die. Ray, I just can't put it into words but I feel you know what I mean. I've lost two weeks work and this may drag on another four weeks.

This all has certainly taught me a lesson. Two weeks of thinking constantly has changed me so much it's hard to believe. I must have been living in another world and now I can look back and see my mistakes in my thinking. It's all changed now. I am hoping and praying constantly that you still want me back. It means a lot to me as you know that, and you will see a different person when I get out. All I want is a chance to forget the past and start anew and you are the only one that can help me. Ray, it means so much to me to be out of here and working, so please do all you can and believe me when I say you and your mom will never regret it.

I just can't seem to eat although there's plenty of food here, and my hip is getting sore again. The same trouble I had before. I worry a lot. I just can't help it, Ray, you know how I am.

Just have faith in me and I'll prove myself. Give my regards to your mom and my best to you.

God Bless you both
Jack

I finished his letter and was trying to sort my thoughts when I heard a knock at my door. It was Ann. I let her read the letter. After she read it she asked, "what are you going to do?"

I shrugged my shoulders, showing my confusion.

"You feel sorry for him, don't you?"

"I'd hate to be the one that makes him go off the deep end."

"Do you believe him?"

"That's the tough part. I've heard his promise's dozens of times."

Ann scanned the letter waiting for my next response. She discussed things, but never imposed her thinking on me. She was wonderfully comfortable to talk to.

"Do you feel you need his help?" She knew I didn't.

"Helen did a great job on me."

"Your Mighty-Mite certainly did." She spread her books on the bedcover. "Do you have any typing paper? I have to draw some exercises and type instructions for speech therapy."

"The typing paper is on the desk. I don't think, Jack will mind if you use his typewriter."

She took several sheets from a pack, then removed the lid from the typewriter.

"There's a sheet of paper in the machine, were you typing?"

"No, it must be Jack's. I haven't touched it for weeks."

She removed the paper, glanced at it, then read silently for a minute. "Oh my God, Ray, you better read this."

The first four lines were gibberish. He must have been one row off on his typing. I smiled and looked at Ann, but her solemn look puzzled me so I read on. The fifth line started,

By and by he will be able to do everything for himself and then where will you be? Shit out in the cold. No more dick, that's what he thinks, he really believes that is the only thing you are starving for, if he only knew that you could have had a lot of men much nicer than him, but he's so conceited and egotistical just like the rest of his fuck'n family that he thinks he's the only thing that matters in the world. These damn Catholics think their shit is holy too. They can fuck all night and confess the next morning and everything is honky dory, that's what they think. But when the final score is tallied they'll all burn in hell as they justly deserve. No wonder he's a cripple. I wonder if he has ever done any deep thinking, and finally found out he is being punished for all his dirty sins, lustful and rapacious as they all are he surely must realize now that in spite of all his praying and the prayers of all the others will be of no avail.

Ann stood silently with her hand on my shoulder. It was difficult grasping the words of a person I thought I knew. I glanced at his letters from jail that were full of "God Bless you. Pray for me. I pray for your forgiveness." Now these words dripping with hate and blaspheme. Ann did not question or comment, she waited for my response. I felt I wanted to yell and swear at him, but could not. Instead I calmly stated. "What turmoil must rage in his head. I have a letter I wrote to him, but I now feel it's best that I cut all ties." I wheeled to the desk and tore the letter into small pieces and threw them into the waste basket.

I looked at her, still not knowing what to say. She sat on my lap, rested her head on my shoulder and we sat silently. I finally said, "type your instructions and I'll help you with the drawings."

Ann was cute as a button with her brunette bangs and impish smile. Her slim build was accented by firm gluts and beautiful legs. Her quads and gastrocks [thighs and calves] were perfectly shaped. Helen taught me muscles and their functions. Humans' simplest of motions became a marvel as I analyzed the scores of muscles that work in unison. To me it was a magnificent symphony, from which I was now excluded.

With Ann, I acted the confident suitor, but inside I wondered what a girl like her could see in me.

Several weeks later, on a beautiful Southern California day, Ann and I were going to the Santa Monica Pier for lunch. As we walked through the lobby, the desk girl motioned to me. She looked unusually serious. "Ray, Jack is here. He had me ring your room and wanted to go up, but I told him he would have to wait in the——. Here he comes now, if you need any help signal me."

I wheeled around.

"Hi, Ray."

Stunned, I tried to find words. I almost said Hi, it's nice to see you're out—or—You're out early. Finally I just said, "hi, Jack."

He looked at the receptionist and Ann, then asked. "Can—we talk privately?"

"Sure."

I excused myself and we went to a couch by the elevator. We shook hands.

"Sit down, Jack."

"I'm sorry to barge in on you like this, but I got an early release yesterday. I picked up the phone a dozen times to call you, but was afraid you'd hang up on me. I couldn't blame you if you did. I had a lot of time to think and pray to God for answers. I'm so sorry for any pain

I've caused you and I've reproached myself a thousand times for leaving you high and dry. Are you okay?"

"I'm okay Jack. Things have worked out. Are you okay?"

"I guess so. I—a—was wondering, could you use me? Just for a while."

I wanted to say sure. But I focused on the paper in his typewriter. I told myself to search for the right words. I was scared clean through.

"Jack, I would like to help you, but I got rid of the big apartment and it's better that I keep learning to do things on my own."

"Ray, I hate talking here in the lobby, I feel like everyone is looking at me. Could we go up to your room and talk?"

The thought of being alone with him frightened me. I felt like I would start shaking any second. I struggled to draw up enough strength, and answered.

"I'm sorry, but I have an appointment, and I'm already late." I looked down at my loafers fearing his next response.

"Well Ray." You have *my* typewriter and tape recorder! I would like them to sell! I *need the money!*"

His humbleness changed to demands, and his change gave me the strength to answer firmly.

"The typewriter cost forty dollars and the tape recorder thirty-five. The wire tape cost ten. I have my checkbook. I'll make you check for a hundred dollars, or if you want your things back, they will be at the desk tomorrow."

He was silent for a long moment, then answered acidly. "I'll take the money!"

I wrote and handed him a check.

"Well, I guess this is it. I wish you all the luck you *deserve*. Remember me in your *prayers*."

I watched his great hulk walk out the door and a wave of relief coursed through my body.

Ann walked next to me, and with her hand on my shoulder, commented, "so that was Jack. He is bigger than I pictured. I was watching his expressions as you talked. What did you say to him before you looked down?"

"He wanted to go to my room and talk, but I told him no. Why?"

"Until then he looked sad and humble, but when you looked down, he glared at you. It was a frightening look. I'm so glad you didn't go with him."

As she pushed me along the boardwalk toward the pier, the sun seemed warmer and the palm trees more beautiful than I remembered. The color of the ocean was blue as my mother's eyes. I looked at my right shoulder. "Thanks for looking after me, Pops. I'm surely glad you and Mom are there to talk to Him, for me."

Ann and I were inseparable and never talked about the time she would leave. Our personal convictions, moral and religious, were the same. I didn't realize until years later how instrumental our special relationship was. I was starting to believe that I *was* someone special, and that women could see past my disability, to whom I really was.

The day she left, I knew we would never meet again.

"The Lord Giveth, and The Lord Taketh Away."

A week later, during therapy, Helen commented, "Ray, you have hit a plateau."

"I believe you're right. I haven't increased my weights in weeks."

"I've pushed you very hard for a year now. The body and mind need a rest once in a while. You have come a *long* way."

"I have come further than I ever dared hope, thanks to you. If someone waved a magic wand to make me walk, I couldn't be happier than I am right now. You have brought me from complete dependence to the sunshine of independence. All the things that people take for granted and do without giving them a thought, like dressing and able to undress by themselves, getting in and out of bed, going to the bathroom, shaving, eating and dozens of little things are now possible for me."

"Ray, you have gained a lot, but I have also. You can only imagine the wonderful feeling I get seeing my efforts result in something worthwhile. I suppose it's like a painter looking at a picture that reflects his soul. I've had a few winners, but you are my best."

We were both near tears when there was a knock at our cubical. A tall, exceptionally handsome man came in and lifted Helen off the floor. He spun her around a couple times, then put her down.

"Ray," Helen giggled, "meet my very good friend, Hank Maginiss. An old college buddie."

His smile was extraordinary and he looked familiar. Helen saw my questioning look.

"Ray, you know him by his movie name, Jeff Hunter."

We shook hands. They talked about college days for a while, then he left.

"He sure is handsome, isn't he? Most of the stars I know are phony, but Hank is one of the few genuine people in the industry."

"I didn't know you knew movie stars."

She smiled. "There are a few things you don't know about me, but back to you. Why don't you take a couple weeks vacation?"

"That sounds like a swell idea. I would like to go home and show off, *the new me.*" I made arrangements to fly home. Robert accompanied me.

He carried me aboard the triple tailed Constellation and put me in a seat next to the window. The propellers changed their pitch cutting deep into the night air, as they pulled our giant silver bird up and away from LAX.

My giant friend slept as we winged East. As we flew over Texas, the sight out my window took my breath away. I had observed the sky countless times, but never saw so many huge, bright stars. So many that the midnight sky was actually white. I was mesmerized by its overwhelming beauty. I then understood what the songwriter saw when he immortalized the words. "The Stars at Night Are Big and Bright, Deep in The Heart of Texas."

We landed in Cleveland. My brother picked us up and we were home after midnight. A dozen family members visited for breakfast. It was great to see everyone and I reveled in their platitudes. The most wonderful feelings came when I saw the happiness in my mother's eyes. It was the first time in five years they showed hope.

After I showed her all the things I could do she broke down and cried. "Your letters were encouraging, but I thought you were just trying to make me feel better. I prayed so hard that you might do at least some of what you wrote. I see now you're better than I dared to dream."

"I'm just starting Mom. I ain't done yet."

Later my brother called me aside. "Marilyn has asked me a thousand times this week when you would be home. She's probably sitting by her window looking over here right now."

I called and said I'd meet her by our garage. I wheeled out in time to see her jump the fence dividing our properties. She ran up, jumped on my lap and cried while we embraced.

"You look great Ray."

"Thanks, and you've changed a lot in a year yourself. Gee. You'll soon be eighteen and legal."

She blushed so easily. I scolded myself for teasing her, but the shyness in her eyes warmed me.

A few days later after things quieted down, Marilyn and I were outside next to my mother's car.

"What are you thinking about Ray?"

"The day I came home from Warm Springs. I was in the living

room looking out the window at mothers' new Cadillac. I cried, telling myself I'd never drive again. I never told anyone, but I always have the same nightmare. I'm driving on a super highway that turns into a smaller road, then to a dirt road, then to no road at all, and I'm trapped in a jungle."

"Don't worry," she consoled. "I'll take you anywhere you ever want to go."

I knew she meant it with all her heart. She continued, "do you think you'll be able to drive someday?"

"I doubt it. My deltoids [shoulder muscles] are dead. How can I steer?"

"Why don't we sit in your mother's car and listen to the music?"

"Okay," I answered. "Would you please get the sliding board off my bed?"

"Sure!"

She ran into the house and was back in a minute. She opened the driver's door and I pulled next to the seat. I removed the right arm of my wheelchair, laid one end of the board on my chair and the other on the car seat and slid over. She moved the chair, shut the door, ran around the car and jumped in next to me.

The feel of the steering wheel was magnificent. I ran my fingers over the ridges on the backside of the wheel and marveled at the beauty of the dashboard, and the long speedometer.

"It's beautiful, isn't it?"

"You look good behind the wheel. Should we go to Lake Erie, or perhaps, Cedar Point?"

"Thanks," I joked. "You know how to hurt a guy."

"Put the radio on Ray, and we can pretend. As long as I'm next to you, we're anywhere we want to be."

I put the radio on, shut my eyes, and with her head on my shoulder we cruised the summer highways.

A sudden impulse jumped into my brain. I turned the ignition key and the powerful smooth engine came to life. It was sweet music to my ears.

Every person has in their brain wonderful memories that are activated by one or more of their senses. Like the smell of popcorn, spring time, a cool crisp fall evening and burning leaves. Perhaps a sound, like a roller coaster, the sound of a summer resort on a warm summer evening. To others, the crack of a bat and a familiar announcer's excitement as he describes a great play.

As a person grows to adulthood, they store vast amounts of special feelings. When these are sensed, the old glorious feelings surge through their body, and transcended them back to those wonderful times.

A polished car, the radio playing "that's My Desire," the windows rolled down letting the sweet smell of summer blow through, and I was on cloud nine.

Another impulse, and I ordered, "sit next to me, and work the gas and brakes. We *are* going for a ride"

"Are you—sure?"

"Yes," I answered confidently. "We have a hundred acres to drive on. All we can do is run over a few plants."

In side, I was really frightened. Not because of the plants I might run over, but that I might find driving impossible for me. As long as I thought there was a chance, I could fool myself. But what if I couldn't drive, could I stand that? I had to know.

"Is your foot on the brake?"

"Yes."

I put the gearshift into "drive" and directed. "Foot off the brake and give it a *little* gas."

The grey coupe started to roll down the driveway toward the back acreage.

"First, we'll practice stopping and starting so you can get the feel of the brakes and accelerator."

We started and stopped a dozen times, and she did her job excellently. We approached the first turn. Now was the hour. I had good strength in my hands and forced the wheel to turn with my wrists. To my surprise and great joy, I made the corner easily.

Confidence surged through my body. "Give it more gas."

"Are you sure? There is a sharp turn ahead."

"I'm sure. Keep it at twenty."

Again, I made it easily.

"*Stop the car!*"

She brought it to a smooth stop.

"I can do it! I *can* drive! Give me a kiss my precious co-pilot."

We drove the dirt roads behind the house for an hour.

"Are you game to cross the highway? We can go to our pond."

"Across Route Twenty?" she exclaimed.

"Why not? Just because I don't have a license and you're working the gas and brakes, what the hell. If we get caught, the poor policeman won't know who to ticket."

I did worry that she might panic in the middle of the road, but I was on a roll and decided to chance it. We stopped at the edge of the highway and waited for a break in the traffic. It finally came.

"*Gas it Marilyn!*"

I must have sounded excited and she floored it. The Coupe DeVille roared across the highway leaving a cloud of dust and two streaks of rubber across the asphalt. We both laughed as we continued down the farm road a half mile to the pond. We were alone, watching the turtles and muskrats at their chores. The windows were down and soft love songs filled the air as we enjoyed our privacy.

During my two weeks we put hundreds of miles on the car driving the farm roads day and night. Marilyn was completely devoted to me, and it was wonderfully flattering. She dated while I was away and told me of her suitors, and one especially that wanted to marry her. I wasn't jealous because she made me feel like I was the only man on earth for her. She gave her love and trust to me completely. She never pushed sex nor denied it.

It was all up to me. Her tall thin body and long shapely legs made sex very tempting, but I was unsure if marriage was inevitable. The world was just restored to me. I felt I could not take advantage of her love. If I started her on intercourse, and didn't marry her, I would feel responsible for betraying her total trust.

The two weeks flew by and I returned to Santa Monica.

CHAPTER FOUR

GREAT LIFE

On the flight back I felt like I was returning to my place of rebirth. I felt warmth as we drove up to the old stone hotel that had been my home for the last year. The greetings I received as I wheeled into the lobby made me feel like I was someone special. I looked down at the huge sitting area and felt like a baby Robin under the safety of its mother's wings. I was in my nest.

At lunch Augie filled me in on the happenings while I was away.

"We have a new group of nurses," he said as he motioned toward the nurses' table. "They're all sitting around the 'old crow'. She watches her brood like a mother hen. See that tall dark haired one? Her name is Jan. We figured you'd match up with her, what do you think?"

"She's okay, but I saw a new blond in the mat class. She is beautiful."

"That's Sara Jane. She's been going with Billy. Poor kid can't make half his classes."

"Billy?"

"Yeah. They're a steady item."

"Lucky guy, she's a knockout."

"You know about Chuck?"

"You mean cool Chuck with his shirt always unbuttoned?"

"Yes. He has a beautiful sweet wife and he takes up with Suzie."

"I know, I was talking to him before I left and he was bragging how he'd be doing Suzie while she was talking to her husband on the telephone. He said he taught his wife about sex and it was now boring with her."

"He doesn't deserve his wife. I hit on her, but she's true blue. What a waste. Anyway, the good news is while you were gone, a vet came in for treatment. He has a brand-new Cadillac convertible and Suzie dropped Chuck. Now he's telling everyone what a slut Suzie is."

"That's great, couldn't happen to a nicer guy. Well, a gotta go. We'll talk later." I wheeled to the tank room and was surprised to see Rob. "Hey big guy, what you doing here?"

"Walley didn't show for work today, so I got switched. Come on, I'll throw you in."

I was on my elbows in the eight-foot tank enjoying the warm water when a brunette walked in.

Not bad looking, I thought. Then she took off her robe. "Oh my God!" I heard myself say as I stared at her huge breasts. She stepped into the tank next to me and saw me staring.

"Hi, you must be new."

"I—a—no, I was home for a couple weeks. I'm Ray. Are you a patient, or just visiting?"

She laughed. "I'm an outpatient. I've been here a couple weeks. I'm Carol."

"You sure look—healthy, for a patient."

"I got a slight case of Polio."

We talked for the half hour. After she left, Rob lifted me to my chair.

"Did you see *those?*" he asked.

"Wow!" is all I could answer.

"I heard Chuck is making a play for her now that, Suzie threw him over."

"Well, Chuck is a good-looking guy and Polio only weakened him temporarily, except in the head."

"Yeah, I made a pass at his wife. No luck. I'd hate to see him score with big tits."

I felt the same. I went to my room, changed and went to the cafeteria for a cup of coffee and a cigarette. Carol was there.

I'm not sure whether it was her build, looks or the challenge with Chuck that prompted me to make a play. Whatever it was, she was receptive and we began dating.

A few days later Suzie stopped me in the hall.

"I hear you're going with Carol. That's great. Chuck's making a play for her and I'm glad to see big mouth get shot down."

I didn't want to discuss personalities so I changed the subject. "I hear you're going home soon."

"Yes, I'm being released next week. I am going to miss the place."

Sure, I thought. *I know what you'll be missing.* To her I said, "yes, there is a great bunch of people here. Will you be an outpatient?"

"For a while I guess," she said, lowering her eyes. "But it won't help, I have a weak ankle."

"Gee, you walk great."

"Well yes, but I won't be able to wear high heals to dance anymore. Just thinking about it drives me crazy. I love to dance."

I struggled to keep a straight face. I couldn't understand how she could stand there, in front of a person like me, and complain about not being able to dance in high heals. But to her, I said, "You're good looking and have a nice figure. People won't even notice you're dancing in flats."

She struggled a smile. "I guess I'll just have to learn to live with it."

I had to leave before I puked. "I'm late for class, I gotta scoot. Good luck."

As I wheeled away I looked up, "Boss, sometimes I just don't understand."

The next morning I heard a knock at my door. I had my pants and socks on, ready to be helped to sit up.

"Come in, Rob." I yelled.

The door opened and Carol stuck her head in.

"Surprise! Rob almost ran me over in the lobby. He said he was late and had to sit you up. I told him I'd do it. Do you mind?"

"Of course not, come on in. Besides, your much better looking."

"Thank you sir."

She sat on the edge of the bed. One thing led to another and we played games. An hour later I said, "gee, I missed Occupational Therapy."

"I don't know about that. You've been very busy."

"You're right. You make a good therapist. We'll have to do this again."

"When?" She asked with a wink.

She held my hand and helped me sit up, then left.

I washed, shaved and conversed with myself in the mirror. "Wow! She is hot. This time, no more chickening out.

For the next two weeks I got a lot of personal Occupational Therapy. Then, disaster struck Saturday morning with a knock at my door, I opened it.

"Good morning, are you Raymond Youdath?"

"Yes I am, Father."

"Is my information correct that you are Catholic?"

"Yes."

"Would you like to receive the sacraments tomorrow?"

"Yes, thank you Father."

"Good."

Then the question that strikes fear in the bravest of souls.

"When was the last time you went to confession?"

My heart sank.

"A few, months ago."

"Well, I have time right now."

I couldn't lie to a priest.

The following Saturday he stopped again to hear confession, again I couldn't lie. That night Carol and I went next door for dinner and then back to my room. She finally asked, "What's wrong? For two weeks you were a passionate fireball, and tonight."

"I don't know. Maybe we better cool it."

"Cool It, not on your life. You can't leave me this hot."

She started her sex act.

At first I told myself, why not? Then those old thoughts tore into my brain again.

"What will you tell the priest next Saturday? What if she gets pregnant? How would your mother feel? She has sacrificed so much to send you here, and you reward her by knocking up a girl. You've saved yourself more than twenty years. Should this girl be the first? Then Marilyn's smile jumped into my mind."

Carol, stop! We can't do this."

It took her a few minutes to regain her composure and asked. "Where do you get the self control?"

The next Sunday was Easter Sunday and we went to my friend's parent's house for dinner. She wore an orchid dress with shoes to match and she looked lovely. My friend's house was an hour's drive from the institute. After we ate, I decided to lie down and rest before we started back. My friend had a great stereo system in his room and I enjoyed Beethoven while I rested and drifted off to sleep. The music was giving me unusually good feelings that woke me. I found Carol opened my pants.

"What the hell are you doing? I can hear Bill's parents doing the dishes."

"That makes it more exciting and you feel it too, I can tell."

She was right and I was tempted, but again my old fears filled my mind and compelled me to say, no, again.

"Damn it Ray, I won't commit you to anything, just satisfy my craving."

"I—can't, I'm sorry."

"Are you worried I might get pregnant?"

I grabbed at that.

"That is a worry."

"I'm regular as clockwork. I was only off once in my life and that was because I was pregnant."

"Pregnant?" I answered, in shock.

I hid my surprise at how casual she was.

"It was at the high school prom. My date put something in my drink. I never knew I was pregnant until I missed my second period."

She smiled jokingly and continued. "My first time and I can't remember a thing."

Stunned and not knowing what to say, I waited, and she continued. "Our parents decided to give the baby up to adoption. I don't even know if it was a boy or girl. I guess my parents were wise about that. When I would feel blue, I couldn't focus on a sex, so the memory faded. Do you think less of me?"

"Of course not. It wasn't your fault."

It was all too confusing and complicated. I wasn't ready for a serious relationship, and I knew if we became sexually involved, it would be serious. We saw each other a few times after that and I was happy we parted friends.

Two Sundays later after receiving communion I wheeled to the cafeteria and picked up a tray.

"Good morning Ray."

"Top'a the morning, Irene. How's my favorite Irish beauty?"

"Cooking away like always. The usual?"

"You bet. It's my favorite meal of the week."

She smiled and poured my coffee. I'll bring your food when it's ready."

"Thanks Irene."

There were ten tables and the only one occupied was the nurse's table. I waved good morning and sat at a table facing them. I was sipping my steaming coffee when Irene set my breakfast on the table.

"Two-two-Four," she said. "Two eggs, two pancakes and four strips of crispy bacon."

"You never forget."

"How can I? You've ordered the same breakfast for a year."

"I guess I'm a creature of habit. Thanks sweetheart."

I attacked my meal like a starving lumberjack. I was on my last strip of bacon when my attention was drawn to a loud crash. I looked toward the entrance as the swinging doors bounced off the walls. Through them rolled "Big Bill." His arms hung lifelessly at his sides and his front castor wheels chattered from the speed. He had a 'shit eaten' grin as he sucked whiskey through a straw from a glass in his right shirt pocket. His left pocket was soaked from sloshing ginger ale. He rolled smack into the nurses' table. More booze and mix spilled over his Hawaiian shirt. He belched, then slurred. "Good morning girls, and especially you, Nurse Parker."

The five student nurses strained to keep from laughing out loud. But Nurse Parker was livid.

"How dare you come in here drunk, and on the Sabbath?"

"Aw—. Is it Sunday already?"

"You! You!—Wait till I speak to Doctor H. tomorrow. Come girls. This is not for you to see."

Bill sat bobbing his head and sucking on his straws. Finally, two of his friends snuck in slowly to make sure Nurse Parker was gone, then they pushed their shirt-soaked friend to my table.

"Mind if we sit with you Ray."

"No, just don't leave him here if he gets sick."

"Don't worry," answered Bill in a sober voice. "I'm not bombed. I just like to shake up that frustrated old bitch."

One of his friends added, "I was afraid to push him in, but you know how nutty he can be."

Irene brought Bill a cup of coffee, a straw and a towel. "When will you ever grow up, Donald?"

"When you tell me, you'll marry me."

She walked away laughing.

"There's gonna be hell to pay tomorrow," I predicted.

"What can they do to me that Polio hasn't already done?"

"You sure got Parker pissed."

"If she only knew that two of her brood got smashed with us last night. As for the Doc, he's cool. I've talked to him before. He understands the patients."

"You'd think Parker would understand as long as she's been around."

"Ray, some women aren't meant to be 'Angels of Mercy.' If I could talk to her for an hour."

"You're a good disc jockey and can bullshit your listeners, but that woman will tear you a new asshole."

"She just needs a good—Oops, careful with your language. Here comes Amie. God damn, she is beautiful."

Amie whipped her green leather chair up to the cashier. Her short, light brown hair was always perfectly groomed. Her pedals were high off the floor indicating her petite size. She balanced her wide ceramic coffee cup on the seat of her chair next to her leg and wheeled toward the next table. As she passed, she smiled. Her full red lips parted showing her perfect white teeth.

"Good morning, boys."

We all answered in our best mannered voices.

"Would you like to sit with us?" one of the boys asked.

"Thank you for the offer, but Irene and Betsy are on their way down."

Every male and female in the institute liked and respected her. I had been to many parties and *never* saw a guy, drunk or sober, make a crude comment to her. A few minutes later her two roommates arrived. She had ordered for them and Irene brought their breakfast.

For the first time since I knew Bill, he began talking seriously.

"You know. I just can't figure it out. Take a young person like, Amie or you, Ray. For God's sake, neither of you are old enough to have done bad things in life. Me, I deserve anything I get. Before Polio, I was a rotten son of a bitch. I made big money as an announcer and was always drunk or high. I fucked anything that walked or crawled and didn't give a shit for anyone. That Guy upstairs sure has things mixed up."

We sat in awe while he stared into space for a moment, then flashed his toothy smile.

"Cheeze, I sound like a preacher. Bob, push me up to my room, I have to change my shirt. Next time I'll bring my soap box."

Bob winked at me as they left.

Amie asked me to join them, then asked. "You all looked like you were in deep thought, and why was Bill all wet?"

I explained what happened, then finished with, "and he said a nice young couple like you and I should get together."

She smiled, giving one of her noncommital answers. "That might not be a bad idea."

"Irene," I asked. "How is that new Victoria running?"

She held her hand to her paralyzed jaw to help her speak. Though difficult to understand at first, you soon understood her perfectly. "Great, I haven't been beaten from a stop light yet."

Amie sighed. "We can vouch for that, can't we Betsy?"

"Oh my God, we sure can.," Josie added. "Whatever you do Ray, never ride with her if it's foggy."

"Whatever do you mean?" defended Irene. "That fog last night wasn't much."

"Wasn't much!" Amie exclaimed. "You couldn't see two feet in front of the car and when you came to a cross street at the same time other car did, you would stop for an instant, then take off."

"Why not?" Irene laughed. "Everyone stops to see what the other car is going to do so I go. Hell, that's nothing compared to Big John and Little John."

"What happened to them?" I asked. They are two Southern boys from the same town that went to Korea and were both shot in the back. They were paralyzed from the waist down.

Big John, a favorite uncle type, was tall, slim and his greying hair gave him distinction.

Little John was shorter with big blue eyes and dark hair. They were both great guys, but would occasionally drink too much.

Amie told the story. "They were celebrating and decided to go for a drive. Big John distracted the night girl at the lobby desk while little John snuck the keys to the institute's car. They had a gallon of Vino and sat in the car listening to the radio until the bottle was empty. Then they decided to go for a ride. Big John took the wheel and Little

John got on the floor to work the gas and brakes."

Irene cut in, "and your ribbing me about my driving."

"Go on," I prompted.

"In their condition Little John misunderstood his orders. He would hit the gas when he was supposed to apply the brakes and vice versa. They were on the road for an hour and damaged twenty-eight cars before their car quit running."

"Twenty-eight!" I exclaimed.

"Yes, and it was a miracle no one was injured. The property damage was tremendous. Luckily, the Government took care of everything."

"Where are they now?"

"They got some bruises and they're at Vallejo. They'll be back next week."

"Wow! You all had a busy time while I was gone. How about you, Betsy, any new adventures?"

She had just opened her pill box. "Dr. H. added four more pills for me to take."

"Four more, how many does that make?"

"Thirty-nine, twice a day."

She put a pile in her hand and took them all in one swallow. Betsy was an attractive thirty year old and always pleasant. Though she tried to hide it, you could tell each movement was painful. Rheumatoid arthritis had devastated her body. Movement in every joint was greatly reduced. Her ankles were swollen from lack of movement.

Irene said. "We are going up the boardwalk to listen to a Jamaican band. Do you want to go, Ray?"

"No thanks, I have a letter to write."

"The girl next door?"

"Actually, yes."

Betsy rocked herself back and forth to gain momentum, then holding on to the edge of the table pulled herself to a standing position.

"Wow," she said with pride. "I made it the first try."

They said good bye. Amie and Irene wheeled slowly next to Betsy. Each step was a three-inch shuffle.

As I watched the slow procession, I told myself, "Raymond, you are luckier than you know."

A hand control salesman said he could custom make me a set of driving controls and teach me to use them. My mother purchased a 1955 Oldsmobile which she and my brother drove to Santa Monica. Before my experience with Marilyn driving a car, I had resigned myself to never drive again. When I saw the beautiful turquoise convertible arrive, I cried like a baby.

It took two weeks to fit the special controls. I had some use of my left leg, so a knee brake and left foot gas pedal were installed beside the regular hand controls. I needed all the help I could get to handle a car. The car had to be finished plus I had to get a driver license before my family left. I feared the driver's test. I had driven with the new set up several times and didn't do well. If I failed to get the license, the car would have to be returned to Ohio. Two days before their flight my brother took me to the license bureau. I easily passed the written test, then got into the car and waited anxiously for the driving test. The agent came out, sat in the back seat and my brother sat next to me. I was instructed to pull out and turn right at the next traffic light. There was a bag of groceries in the back seat with a roll of toilet paper on top.

The agent saw it and laughed. "Is this toilet paper for me? Will I need it for your driving?"

"I hope not," my brother answered for me.

I was very lucky to get a nice agent. He instructed me to make three more right turns and stop where we started.

"Okay son, you passed."

To this day I believe it was the toilet paper that got me the driver's license.

The man that installed my controls didn't understand leverage. The rod to the foot brake was too far out on the hand brake. I couldn't push hard enough to lock the brakes and I was afraid to tell anyone for fear they would stop me from driving. The next few weeks were terrifying. I had to analyze traffic and know where every car around me was in case I had to stop fast. I would occasionally pull off the road and chastise myself.

"This is stupid, Raymond. You can't stop this car fast enough. You've been very lucky so far, how many times will God bail you out?"

It didn't take long to start finding the answer to that question.

Eventually I had the fulcrum changed and I was, 'On the Road Again.'

Life was starting to bloom. The very first person to ride in my car was Amie. We drove along the Pacific coast highway through Malibu past all the beach homes. The top was down, the music was romantic and we were part of the beautiful people. Naturally I was looking for a secluded place to park. I spotted a road heading up into the foothills. I started the uphill climb. The road wound around a mountain. We passed many beautiful homes as we climbed higher and higher. The road was narrow and I was getting nervous. The combination of steepness, no guard rails and my inexperience driving told me to turn around. I just passed a wide driveway and decided to let the car coast back and into the drive. As my car-coasted back I did not realize my engine had stalled and the reserve power brake tank was emptying. Suddenly I lost my brakes and power steering. I pushed the hand brake with all my strength to no avail.

"Amie!" I yelled. "My power brakes are gone, help me push the hand brake."

We pushed together. We slowed, but the car kept coasting backwards. I looked in my rearview mirror. I had fifty yards before a sharp turn and we would roll off the edge.

I blocked out Amie's words of fear and ordered myself. "Stay calm, Raymond. You must start the engine and build up a vacuum. Don't look in the mirror again, just concentrate on starting the car. First, take it out of reverse and put it in neutral. Good, now pull yourself forward with your left hand and push the starter button with your right. I know you can't reach it without shoulder muscles, just rest your forearm on your knee. That's it. Now start it. It isn't starting. Pump the gas, but only once. If you flood it—. Now try again. It started! Oh shit! The brakes still don't work. You have to pump them, dummy. No! Don't waste time looking in the mirror, keep pumping. The brake is coming up and starting to grab. PUSH WITH ALL YOUR STRENGTH. We stopped. Now you can look in the mirror. Oh My God, only sky."

Amie was sobbing. "Ray! The back bumper is over the edge and the ground may give away."

To myself, "you're not out of it yet, Raymond. The hand brake is also the gas. You must give it the right amount of gas. Too much and you may stall, too little—and you coast backwards over the edge. Don't waste time thinking negative. First, get it in gear."

"Amie," I said. "Listen carefully. Put the gearshift into drive, the first click down. *Do Not Hit Reverse.*"

"Watch the indicator," I told myself. "She is scared, so talk calmly to her."

"Good girl, that's the correct gear. Amie, if you want to roll out of the car before I try to drive out of this, go ahead."

She half smiled. "I thought of that before, but I couldn't leave you. I figured I could help."

"I wouldn't have had a chance without you."

To myself I said, "you're great, but you should jump out. Well, here goes. Remember, enough gas so the car doesn't roll back. One more foot and you're over the cliff."

I remembered the words I spoke a week earlier. "How many times will He be there?"

He was there again and I pulled ahead safely. Without a word I turned the car around and drove back down the winding road. At the bottom I stopped and shut off the engine. We sat in silence for a half hour. On the way back to the institute I looked up. "No more excitement Boss, I've had enough for a lifetime."

I guess. He must have been busy and didn't hear me. The very next Friday night I drove to a local drive-in theater with a friend. After I dropped her at her home, I drove back to the institute. I pulled up to the entrance and parked heading into the curb. I blew my horn twice, my signal to Arnie, the elevator operator. He came out with my wheelchair. I slid onto it and he helped me onto the sidewalk. The curbs in California are extra high to contain the torrents of water when it does rain. A policeman's three-wheeled motorcycle was parked at the curb next to me. He was inside talking to the girl at the desk.

The street was about sixty feet wide and cars parked on both sides, heading into the curbs at an angle.

Bernie got into my car. He was going to back out into the street, then drive it up the hill to the parking lot, as he had done before. He started the powerful Olds engine, put it into reverse, turned the wheel and started to back up. Bernie had a huge heart and smile, but short legs. I had the seat way back and he forgot to move it forward. When he tried to reach the brake pedal he realized his mistake and reached for my hand brake. His second big mistake.

Instead of pushing he pulled it, which floored the accelerator. The engine roared and the tires screamed. The front wheels were turned and the car flew backwards in a big circle. Poor Arnie froze. One hand griped the steering wheel and the other pulled the hand control. My new turquoise beauty was near rolling over as it made its sharp circle. The right front hit a parked car across the street tearing off my front bumper and the other car's rear bumper. The impact echoed between the institute and the hotel across the street. I was on the curb not believing my eyes. Then my surprise turned to terror as I saw my car making the circle and backing toward *me*. The engine was screaming as clouds of burning rubber filled the street.

I heard the panic in my voice as I yelled out loud. "Back up Ray! Your car will jump the curb and you'll be crushed!"

Before I could move a foot, the right rear wheel hit the high curb right in front of me and bounced the back of the car away from me. Then the right front wheel hit the curb with such force that the impact tore the whole wheel assembly off. The badly wounded machine roared past me dragging the wheelless right front end. I saw Arnie's face. His eyes were locked wide open with terror. He had a death grip on the wheel and the floored hand control. He was in a trance. Then another deafening crash as the rear of my Olds hit the Police three wheeler rolling it over and climbed on top of it. This last impact caused my beauty to hesitate a moment as the back end balanced on the smashed cycle. It rocked side to side trying to reach the pavement so it get traction and continue on its circle of destruction.

I screamed at Bernie trying to break his spell, "Bernie! Take it out of gear! Turn the key off!—Turn the key off!"

Arnie slowly turned his head toward me, still wide eyed and still pulling on the hand control. I knew a couple more rocks and the powerful screaming car would be off again. His eyes finally focused on me and I motioned with my hand to turn off the key. He finally understood and turned the ignition off.

The engine sputtered, then finally became silent, resting on the destroyed motorcycle.

The multitude of sickening reports brought the policeman running out of the institute. He immediately ran to the driver's side and opened the door to check on Bernie, who was still in shock. He had to pry his hand off the wheel and near a carry him into the institute. Poor Bernie couldn't talk for a half hour. All he kept saying was, "I'm sorry, Ray, your nice new car, I don't know what happened."

After the policeman was sure everyone was okay he spoke to me. "Sorry about your new car, I know how you feel. I just got my bike out of the shop today. I'm just retired and I got a contract escorting dignitaries and stars for MGM."

As I watched my battle-scarred friend being towed away, I glanced up. "Thanks for saving me again, Boss. But could you be a little less dramatic next time, please."

At the supper table the next evening everyone expressed their condolences.

Big Bill jibbed. "So you lost your girl for a while."

"Yeah," I answered. "She needs a nose job."

"More than that according to poor Benie. He said he's afraid to drive the elevator now. Two cars and a cop's three wheeler in ten seconds, that's a record."

Chad, a six-foot tall blond with a perpetual smile was being fed by a friend. He injected. "You should have one of my foot controls." Polio laid waste both of Chad's arms. From his waist down he was normal. He invented a round disc mounted left of the brake pedal and hooked to the power steering. With his left foot on the disc he can steer his car.

He continued, "my brother drives my car with his hands cupped behind his head and gets a kick watching people's expression while he maneuvers through traffic."

Big John and Little John joined the group.

Little John started. "I hear Benie is trying to break our record."

Big John added, "that would shore take a heap a try'n, or a heap a drink'n."

Chad nodded. "No one will ever break your record."

"By God, Chad," said Big John. "I think there's a mite big hunk a truth to them words."

"Damn," injected Chad. "I wish Polio had knocked out my legs and left my arms alone. You guys don't realize how lucky you are."

[Us] "You're better off than wheelchair people. You can walk anywhere."

[Him] "No, you're better off. I can walk to a door but I can't open it."

[Us] "Bullshit, a curb can't stop you, and steps can't keep you from a restaurant."

[Him] "Big deal. I can get into a restaurant and order a meal, but I can't feed myself. Moreover, if I gotta take a leak, I have to ask a stranger to unzip my pants and flip it out. Then, if the stranger is too willing, I have to worry he might not let go."

[Us] "Wow! Never thought of that. You win. We are better off."

Then I injected, "wait a minute. Wear a wig, then you can go into the girl's john and your girl can handle it for you."

[Him] "Yeah, not bad. Mix business with pleasure." He flashed his 'apple pie' smile.

"Hold yer horses," Little John cut in. "All you Polio's are better off than a paraplegic."

[Us] "Are you nuts! Paras have normal arms, are independent and don't have to kiss anyone's ass to do anything."

[Them] "True, but we gotta wear diapers. We never know when we're gonna shit ourselves and worse, we can't get a hard on."

[Us] "What good is a hard on if you can't get around to use it?

Sure, if [We] have normal arms then [We] are better off. But, go down to the ward. Nine out of ten Polio's would change places with you in a second."

[Them] "Sure, till they have to live like a Para."

[Us] "Horse manure. You live their lives, then talk."

[Them-Us] "Hey, what the hell are we doing, let's go to the Cork, and get stinko."

Just then Jackie wheeled to our table.

"Stinko! Are you boys telling war stories again?"

I answered, "We're arguing about who's better off with what disability. What do you think?"

She was too smart to answer that question, instead she said, "No, I heard the word 'stinko' and it reminded me of something."

I helped her change the subject.

"Now what would a Canadian girl from the really far north mean by that?"

Big John asked. "Y'all from Canada?"

"Yes, my dad has a trading post near Hudson Bay."

"By golly, my southern bones chill when I even think above the Mason Dixon line."

"Big John, you wouldn't last ten minutes. Our trading post is a hundred miles from the nearest town."

"Lord, girl, who do y'all do business with, big white bears?"

"Sometimes," she laughed. "But mostly with the surrounding tribes."

"Lord A-mighty. What'd y'all do when you got Polio?"

"You really want to know?"

We all answered "yes" at the same time.

"No one knew a thing about Polio and the provincial doctor only flew in once a month. Polio knocked out my right arm and right leg. Luckily I didn't need a respirator."

85

Big Bill asked. "What did you do for treatment?"

"*That* is the *sad* part. Too much advice that damn near killed me."

"Like what?" We asked.

"When Dad's customers found I was stricken with paralysis, they all brought their home cure recipes and my father made me try everyone. Fresh-cut hay boiled in cabbage water. It smelled like manure water, and tasted worse. Then and an old toothless Indian squaw brought in a concoction of boiled and steeped roots. I threw up every time I drank it and I had to drink a glass full a day for a week. Next was some mixture that was induced with an enema tube. I remember thinking nothing in the world could be worse, but boy was I wrong. Late one morning my dad came into my room. "Sweetheart, the medicine man from the Hudson Tribe came in yesterday. He traveled a hundred miles with a sure cure."

"I knew I was in trouble when he called me 'sweetheart'. I told him I would rather die than go on with the 'cures'.

"Sweetheart," he pleaded. "Just one more, I promise."

Stupidly, I agreed. He ran out of my bedroom. Unknown to me, they had killed and skinned a calf.

Within a couple minutes my father and uncle brought in a bloody, still warm, hide to my room. Before I had a chance to protest, they wrapped me in it. Between the slippery blood and hair under my chin, I didn't know whether to throw up, faint or die."

"Remember Sweetheart," my father said apologetically. "This is the last one. The medicine man said it worked many times already."

"I knew my father was trying the best he could so I resigned myself to stick it out. The smell was so repugnant and I couldn't sleep or eat. After the second day my family would run out of the room vomiting. They refused to return and my father had to feed me and attend to my personal needs.

"After a week of vomiting himself, he conceded to end the 'cure'.

"The hide dried so stiff they had to cut it off. The room was impregnated with the foul smell. They had to burn every piece of furniture, including the drapery, clothes and rugs. The entire room was refinished, including the floor. The windows had to be left open in the whole house. Everyone, including me, nearly froze to death. The only good thing that came out of the ordeal was an end to 'home cures'."

Everyone at the table was mesmerized and unable to speak.

She said. "That's what I thought about when I heard the word stinko."

We all admitted none of us could match her ordeal and she was the reigning queen.

Half of the forty rooms in the institute were empty every night because most everyone was sleeping with someone else.

I was disappointed to learn that married people played around the first chance they get.

My car was in the repair shop about two weeks when I went to a party across the hall. I was having a good time socializing.

At the party Amie laughed. "You can always tell when the booze is starting to affect, Ray. He's all smiles."

She was right.

One of the nurse's at the party said, "all the seats are taken. Is your lap available?"

"Of course, at your own risk."

"You sound dangerous. Can I trust you?"

"Of course not."

"Good," she cooed, then sat on my lap.

We talked, joked and I got a couple kisses for supplying a seat. After she left, a girl I didn't know spoke to me.

"Hi, my name's Paula. Is your lap still available?"

"Be my guest Paula." She sat, and I continued, "You have beautiful blue eyes."

"Thank you, all I need is blond hair."

"Why in the world would you want blond hair."

"Because everyone wants a blue-eyed blond."

"Naw, that's ordinary. You're different. Black hair and blue eyes, who can forget you."

"My boyfriend never says nice things like that."

"Then it's time for a new boyfriend."

She was a bit tipsy and I enjoyed the game. Try to figure out what they like to hear and say it. She said she would like to meet me at a bar in Santa Monica some evening. "Sure," I told her, but I knew I wouldn't. I wasn't comfortable in the "outside" world.

Later, I was talking to Amie and tried to kiss her.

"Sorry Ray, not here. If a girl let's a couple guys kiss her at a party, she loses control. If you kiss one guy and refuse another, they get angry. Then you're always fighting off the jerks."

I listened as intently as I could. Very philosophical I thought, but much too deep tonight.

"Besides being beautiful, you're also smart," was the best I could come up with.

"Later," she said.

I mixed another drink and was enjoying the music when someone said, "Good thing you don't have far to drive home."

I looked over my shoulder.

"Hi Linda, I didn't see you come in."

"I just got here. Timmy was uncomfortable from treatment. They fit him with a brace today and worked him very hard."

"You have a good-looking son. He'll be running all over before long."

"Thanks for the compliment. He did very good today. The doctor said he'd be out of the chair in a couple more weeks."

"That's great, Linda. You better get a drink quick if you want to catch up."

As she walked away, I studied her body. About five foot five I guessed. She had strong calf muscles and a super set of gluts. She and her son had been at the institute a month. As she returned, I watched her silk shirt move back and forth over her body. Lucky brother, I thought. She sat next to me and we continued talking. I enjoyed her southern accent.

"I understand you have horses," I commented.

"Actually we'all breed and train them for clients, but that's not unusual in the Blue Grass state."

"Is that how you stay so, trim?"

"It does help. Staying on a ton of muscle at a full gallop does take *special* muscles."

I tried not to look surprised as I wondered if she meant what I thought she meant.

"You and your brother are a lot alike. I felt you studying me as I walked away. Then you undressed me as I walked back, did you like what you saw?"

I felt electricity run down my spine. I was way over my head with this conversation.

To myself I said, "what are you gonna say now, wise guy? If she knew how little experience you've had, she would be talking to someone else. But she doesn't know and must think I'm like my brother, so, what the hell. Say what she wants to hear."

I answered her question like I knew what I was saying. "You know I did."

Just then the blue-eyed brunette walked up and asked. "Is your lap still available?"

Linda answered for me. "Sorry Paula, his dance card is full."

With that she sat on my lap and Paula left.

"You don't mind, do you?"

"Hell no. I always wondered what gluts that can conquer a two thousand-pound thoroughbred would feel like."

"Gee Raymond, all you had to do, was whistle."

She put her fingers to my lips forcing them to pucker and kissed me like I had never been kissed before. A wave of heat coursed through my entire body.

"Wow," she whispered. "You do remind me—. Did you know I was seeing your brother?"

"He mentioned you spent some time together and he enjoyed your company."

"Are there any more handsome brothers in your family?"

"No, he's the only one.

"What are you talking about? I think you're handsome."

"Naw. I might not break any mirrors, but I don't come close to him."

"My-my, and he's modest too."

I tried to control myself, but her movements were making it impossible.

She continued, "I'm glad to—see that I am having an effect on you."

Raymond, I thought. *Be careful.*

At that bewildering moment her son's physical therapist approached. "Hi Ray. Linda, can I talk to you for a minute about Timmy?"

"Sure Bill. Excuse me Ray, just keep that thought."

They went to a quiet part of the room and sat on a couch. I knew Bill had the hots for her, and anyone else in a skirt.

I was thankful for the intercession.

Augie, Amie and Jackie walked next to me. "We were waiting to talk to you about the club room."

Amie added, "Actually, we were waiting for you to come up for air."

Augie added. "We talked to Miss Anderson this afternoon about the room you suggested in the basement next to the elevator. She talked to Dr. H. and he okayed it, but first he wants to talk to you in the morning."

"Yeah, Miss A was afraid he might say no because there would be drinking."

Jackie smirked. "She really went to bat for you with the Doc. I think she likes you."

"She reminds me of my favorite aunt. As Recreation Director, she just wants a happy community."

Jackie finished with, "I don't think she thinks of you as a favorite *nephew*."

I thought that was a dumb thing for her to say. The director was a very nice lady. While we continued small talk about furniture and ground rules, I noticed Linda getting a drink. She glanced toward us, then returned to Bill and a couple people that joined their group.

I knew I had enough to drink and decided to call it a night.

"Well girls and boys, I better rest for my talk with our illustrious doctor in the morning."

I said my good byes and wheeled across the hall to my room. As I passed my mirror I spoke to my image, as I always did. "What's that shit eaten grin for? Think your cool? Well, I must admit, for a tall skinny guy in a wheelchair, you don't do *too* bad. Okay smiley, go to bed and try not to fall off your sliding board, and remember to put the orange on your night stand. You know how thirsty you get when you've been drinking."

I put my shirt and corset over the back of my wheelchair then parked next to the bed. I pulled my pants half off, slid the board under my butt and slid onto the mattress. I removed my trousers and hung them over my corset. I checked to make sure everything was in place for morning. I grabbed my knee, rocked back onto the bed and pulled the covers over myself. I rested my head on the pillow and said, "thank you Helen."

I pulled out the plunger on my alarm, shut off the light on my night stand and started my evening prayers.

"Sorry I can't get on my knees, Boss. But say the word and I will. Well, if your busy tonight, maybe tomorrow night."

I finished my prayers and was smiling to myself thinking of the day's activities when I heard my door close softly. I opened my eyes and with the dim light that filtered in my window I saw a figure walking toward me and asked, "who's there?"

"It's just little ol' me," Linda answered.

"You startled me."

As she undressed she said. "We didn't get a chance to finish our conversation."

Within a minute she was standing naked next to my bed. She stood still long enough to make sure I had time to feast my eyes on her body.

"My God," I heard myself say out loud. "You are, beautiful."

"Well thank you, kind sir."

She pulled my covers off and laid them on the chair, sat on the bed and kissed me. Her tongue darted into my mouth as the smell of her perfume further overwhelmed me.

My hands explored her magnificent body and I felt the strong contractions of her gluts.

"Damn," I thought. "If I had those muscles I could jump over a car." I laughed to myself. "Jesus, Ray. Do you always have to think about muscles?"

She moaned as she said, "This—gives—a—WHOLE—new—meaning—to—keeping—it—in—the—family."

Then again, my nemesis kicked in.

"Raymond, what the hell are you doing? Have you forgot what your mother is sacrificing for you? What if Linda gets pregnant? You've been saving yourself for twenty-five years. Is this the time and girl? Hell yes, you stupid shit. Don't chicken out again. This is the perfect time for crying out loud, you're three thousand miles from home. Do it and worry tomorrow.

But, she's married, and you always criticize married people that play around.

Damn it Ray, you only went to the fifth grade in Catholic school. Why do you have such a conscience?"

Then I heard myself say out loud those darned old words. "I can't do this."

I had to repeated it louder. "I CAN'T DO THIS!"

She ignored me again.

"LINDA, I'M SORRY. I CAN NOT DO THIS. PLEASE STOP."

"I can't Ray. Just relax and enjoy. I promise a night you'll never forget."

I panicked. "What the hell did you start Ray? Think of something to say. You can't stop her physically. Ray, this is not what you want."

I thought of something and said, "Linda, the only problem is Amie."

"Amie? She'll never know."

"That's the problem. We are so close, we tell each other everything."

"You mean you'd tell her about this?"

"I'm afraid I might."

She stopped and stood up. She turned and looked down at me. "Too bad my friend, we almost made it to the moon."

She dressed, leaned over and kissed me lightly. "Raymond, I've never met a man with your willpower. I don't like it exactly, but I do respect it. Good night. I hope you have a miserable night sleeping. I know I will."

She turned and left. I lay in the darkness puzzled with myself. Why, I don't know, but the words of an old song I learned in grade school came to me. We sang it every May.

"On this day, O Beautiful Mother, on this day we give The' our love, near The' Madonna, fondly we hover, trusting thy gentle, care to prove."

I drifted off to sleep seeing myself and my classmate skipping around the May Pole.

I didn't leave my door unlocked again.

CHAPTER FIVE

OUT OF COCOON

At breakfast the next morning a good looking new speech therapist setting with us saw Robert in the breakfast line. "My God!" she exclaimed, oblivious of all around her. "Who is that? I never thought of cheating, but he could change my mind."

She shocked us all. But, sunny California is a world unto itself.

His white teeth contrasted his deep tan.

"Morning, everyone."

His six-foot seven frame dwarfed the cafeteria chair as he sat holding his steaming cup of coffee.

"Hey Rob," I started. "We're all anxious to hear about your screen test yesterday."

He retained his perpetual smile. "I never went."

"You never went! To a screen test at MGM, are you nuts?"

"Hey," he said, as he feigned a serious facade. "What would my friends in 'Dago' think if I let a little guy like Alan Ladd knock me down? I'd never be able to show my face. They'd laugh me out of town."

"Robert," I continued. "People give their souls for a screen test, and you just don't show up?"

"Ray, you just don't understand. Guys a foot shorter than I, knocking me down! I have a reputation to uphold."

He laughed along with the rest of us. He probably used the opportunity to get out of the house to meet some girl. We all knew he was a philanderer, but you couldn't help liking him. He turned the simplest thing into a hilarious story.

"Meet you in the pool at ten. Got stuff to tell ya." The therapist looked at him in a trance as he walked away.

After my eight o'clock therapy with Helen, I met with Dr. H. I showed him the rules we would live by in our new clubroom. He left no doubt that it would be closed immediately with the first infraction. My next class was pulleys. I was next to Augie as the instructor checked our charts and attached our proper weights.

"What did the administrator say?" Augie asked.

"If we fuck up, even once, no more clubroom."

Authors' note: The clubroom was used every night. Card games, reading, socializing and scores of parties. The Recreation Director received an accommodation for our perfect record, which we displayed proudly.

After pulleys I went to Pool Therapy. The Institute, an ex-Luxury hotel, had an Olympic sized pool. Rob's lifeguard credentials secured him the pool director's position. He sat me on the edge of the pool, then into the water. At 6'7" his body rippled with protruding muscles and in perfect proportions. I guess that's why his mood was always mellow. He never had to *act* tough. He attached weights to my ankles and we went to the five-foot depth and he held my hand as we walked back and forth a dozen times.

"God," I thought. "How I love the water. The buoyancy allows my trace muscles to move my limbs full range. If the U.S. got a colony on the moon, I'd sign up immediately. The low gravity would allow me to walk with crutches."

Rob interrupted my pleasant daydreaming. "Ray, I got an invitation to a party in the canyon, and I can bring a guest. Do you want to go?"

We had double dated before. He would lift me in the backseat and we would go to drive-in movies, drive-in restaurants and drives along the ocean. But never to regular theaters or restaurants.

"Well Ray. How about it?"

"I-aa, when is it?"

"Saturday night."

"Oh shit, I already made plans. Maybe next time." I lied.

I was afraid to go out in public among able-bodied people.

The following Monday as we walked in the pool he said, "Wow! You missed a great party."

"How was it?"

"I drove up a long drive that wound deep into a canyon. Halfway up was an armed guard that checked my invitation and driver's license. Christ, I thought. Must be a lot of rich shits with expensive jewelry.

I drove another half mile to a sprawling mansion.

There were Rolls, Jags, Caddies and little foreign jobs, and me with my little old Chevy. I told the parking attendant to be careful parking my car. He smiled, I asked him what was funny. He near shit when I got out. He looked up at me and quickly directed me to the archway entrance. I got to the front gate and two gorgeous, naked girls said, "your clothes please."

"My clothes!" I exclaimed.

"No shit. They helped me undress and tied a ticket around my wrist. They told me not to lose the ticket, then they started undressing the next couple. I walked into this giant area in the middle of the villa. A two-story fountain had at least a dozen naked men and women splashing around. They were screwing all over the place. On the floor, chairs, couches and even the stairs. Front wards, backwards, sideways and upside down. Black, White, Oriental, Spanish and others. Girls and girls, guys and guys and groups that were so tangled I couldn't figure who was doing what to whom. A bald guy with rolls of fat and a monkey on his shoulder greeted me. His belly hung so low, I couldn't even tell if he had a dick."

"Welcome my giant hunk of love," he said. "Who was lucky enough to invite you?"

"Mary Ann."

"That bitch. Keeping the big ones for herself. Oh well, Mandrake and I will mingle with the guests. Tell Mary Ann, I hope her big tits fall off."

"I was ready to smash the slob and leave when two beautiful Oriental girls invited me upstairs for a rub down. "What a night. I got shit faced and the next thing I knew I woke up in my car at the bottom of the long drive with my clothes next to me. Next time I'll stay sober so I can remember what I did. What do you think Ray, you want to go next time? And don't worry, I saw a couple girls and a guys in wheelchairs."

The thought that I *almost* went, scared me.

"If I were built like you."

He laughed. "Bull shit, you're just chicken."

He was right.

My next class was occupational therapy. I was making a box for a nickel plated Western 45 revolver

I was sanding away when Dr. H. called my name. "Ray, I'd like you to meet Mrs. Blackman and her mother."

We shook hands and he continued. "Her brother has M.S. and they are checking out our facilities.".

I talked to the mother while the doc explained the occupational therapy department.

"Ray," the doctor asked, "we are going to the cafeteria, would you like to join us?"

I was tempted, but I declined. "Thanks, but I better finish my project. We start on the looms tomorrow."

"See," he said proudly. "Our patients enjoy their work."

We shook hands and they left. I figured they must be important for the doc to give them a personal tour. A half hour later patients and therapists were all gathered talking excitedly.

"What's going on?" I asked.

"What's going on? Did you see *her?*"

"Did I see *who?*"

"Shirley Temple."

"Shirley Temple. Wow, where is she?"

"She's with Dr. H."

"I just saw him. He's with a woman named Blackman."

"You dummy. That's her married name. Shirley Temple Blackman."

"What! I had a chance to eat with Shirley Temple and I turned it down."

I wheeled to the cafeteria as fast as I could, but she had left. Dejected, I started drowning my sorrows in a cup of coffee.

"Hi, Ray."

I looked up. "Hi, deltoids."

Jill was a nice girl about sixteen. She liked the nickname I gave her, and she proudly flexed her shoulder muscles.

"Jealous?" she taunted.

"Yes. You want to sell them?"

"Ha! You'll be the first to know. By the way, did you see Shirley Temple. She just left the cafeteria."

"Yes," I moaned. "I saw her."

"Ray, I've been invited to my uncle's house for supper tonight and they told me to bring a friend, would you like to go?"

"Gee thanks Deltoid, but my mom's calling tonight about the insurance on my car."

I lied. I was still brooding about Shirley Temple.

About ten that night I went down to the lobby to mail a letter. While waiting for the elevator, Deltoid came in with her aunt and uncle and they got on the elevator with me. Her aunt was dressed most elegantly and her uncle stood next to me. I glanced at his plaid sport coat. It was brilliant shades of green.

"That's a beautiful sport coat," I commented.

"Why thank you," he returned.

Then Deltoid said, "Ray, I'd like you to meet my aunt Glenda and uncle Robert."

I looked up as I shook his hand and damn near fell out of my chair. It was Robert Young. The elevator door opened and they left.

I sat in a stupor as the elevator automatically proceeded to the eighth floor. The doors opened and closed and I wound up down on the first floor again. The door kept opening and closing.

"What a day you've had, stupid. First you refuse to sit with Shirley Temple, then you refuse to go to Robert Young's house for supper. This has got to be the dumbest day of your life."

The next morning, looking in the mirror while shaving, and continued chastising myself. "Ray, you *have* to go out in public. You can't keep turning down invitations. Who knows, you might have had a chance to be in a movie with Robert Young, you never know.

You talk cocky, then piss out. Aw-w shut up and get to P.T."

I wheeled into Helen's cubical and was surprised to find a girl on the table.

"Come in Ray. We'll be done in a minute. Dr. H wanted me to give this girl an evaluation. Ann, this is Ray. Ray, this is Ann."

We exchanged formalities, then Ann continued. "Sorry to interfere in your therapy."

"No problem," I answered. Helen finished the muscle check then wrote on the girl's chart. Ann sat up using her arms, pulled her chair next to the table, positioned her legs and with one hand on the table and the other on the opposite arm of her chair and glided onto the seat.

Without thinking I exclaimed out loud. "Damn, that was quick." She smiled as she adjusted her slacks and blue sweatshirt.

"Thanks, Helen and thanks for your time, Ray. It was a pleasure meeting you both."

"Take this chart to Dr. H."

She whipped her chair around me and disappeared through the curtain.

Helen answered my thoughts. "Wish you had arms like that?"

"Wow! She was up and in her chair in five seconds. Are you going to be her therapist?"

"No. The Doctor assigns me the challenging cases, like you. She has normal arms and trunk, but her legs are gone. They'll build her upper body with mats and pulleys."

"She reminds me of Joan Crawford, and she's very articulate."

"She should be, she's an Ivy league graduate."

"That's it."

"What's it?"

"Her mannerism emanates self confidence. I should have gone to college."

"I always assumed you did."

"Dad died the year I was going to Ohio State. I waited a year, then Polio nailed me."

After pulley class I mailed a letter then wheeled into the cafeteria for a cup of coffee. I spotted the new girl and a woman I assumed was her mother.

As I wheeled by, I said. "Good morning girls."

They asked me to join them, I did and Ann introduced me to her mother.

"Welcome to Santa Monica and C.R.C." I said.

"Thank you Ray. It does seem to be a nice place."

"I've been here for a year and gained more than I ever dreamed. Doctor Huddleson, in my opinion, is the finest in the world and the staff is unbeatable."

"Are you telling us you like the place?"

"Yes, I guess I am."

Her mother commented. "We weren't sure until we checked the facility. Ann has decided to stay for treatment. I'm flying home today and will drive her car out next week."

"Great," I said. I knew they had things to discuss. "I have to get to my next class. Nice to meet you and I look forward to seeing you again. Drive carefully."

I left thinking I was too corny, but I guess not. At supper that night Ann asked me if I like Beethoven.

I was going to say Bee-who? But just answered, "yes."

She invited me to her room to hear a new record she bought.

I knocked at her door at eight sharp. Her room reminded me of college rooms I'd seen in movies. Piles of books, a record player with several speakers, a typewriter, alarm radio, banners and an open suitcase that was a well stocked bar. I felt way over my head and was afraid to talk for fear I'd show my illiteracy.

Her easy manner and soft voice soon had me at ease. She didn't flaunt her Ivy league education and apparent wealth, which impressed me. The only classical music I knew was The William Tell Overture, thanks to The Lone Ranger. And my favorite dancing song [pre Polio] was Opus # Five.

I stayed until eleven and we shook hands as I thanked her for a very pleasant evening.

As I wheeled back to my room, I thought of the dumb things I said and smart things I should have said.

In my room, I stopped in front of my mirror to hear my evening comments. "Ray, if that girl finds you interesting, you better worry about her sanity."

We spent a lot of time together that week. Her mother arrived on Friday with her blue Olds and they invited me to dine with them on Sunday. After I accepted, I chastised myself.

"You dummy. What are you gonna wear? You can't wear worn loafers, white socks and a turquoise sweater to a classy restaurant on the Sunset Strip."

Robert drove me to a men's store and I bought a sport coat, trousers, shoes and dark socks.

Back in my room I talked to my confidant, the mirror. "Why didn't you just refuse? Everyone in the restaurant will be staring at you. First, because you're in a chair and you can't eat normally. Your left hand has to help your right get the food to your mouth. And *don't* order soup. Your stupid weak wrist turns in and you'll spill soup on your shirt. Oh God, why did you accept. You'd be happier going to a drive in restaurant." I glanced around. "You better be careful talking to yourself in a mirror. Someone will toss a net over you yet."

I picked up the phone a hundred times to cancel. Finally, the day arrived. Ann and her mother were dressed conservative, yet elegant, and I felt like a clod. They drove. The valet parked the car and her mother had to help push me up the ramp while Ann sped ahead and opened the door.

"Great service," I said jokingly, trying to cover my hurt. I should be opening the door for them.

Then the menu. I didn't recognize any of the entrees, so I ordered what they did.

I did decline soup. It was the only smart thing I did. They brought a huge bowl of salad that was mixed at the table. Pretty fancy I thought. We started on the salad.

"This dressing is good," I said to them. Then to myself, "try not to drip it on your tie. Hmmm, bacon. Never saw bacon in salad before, especially with little hairs. So what do you know anyway. You never ate in a fancy restaurant before. I saw them eating the 'bacon' and they commented how tasty it was, so I popped one in my mouth. I took two bites and my system registered 'tilt,' and I said to myself. "What is this? It is terrible, what am I going to do with it? I can't spit it out and if I swallow it, I'll probably throw up. Try not to show a reaction."

But it was too late.

"Are you all right Ray?" Ann asked.

I tried to smile with a mouthful of, I knew not what. I had to decide fast. I grabbed the wine glass, took a big mouthful and swallowed. Two more gulps and my eyes returned to their sockets.

I pointed to a piece in my salad and with tears in my eyes asked, "what is this?"

Ann laughed. "Anchovies, a type of fish. You have to develop a taste for their saltiness."

Salt on shit I felt like saying. Instead I answered graciously. "Yes, the salt was a bit stronger than I expected."

"Mother and I will share the rest if you don't enjoy them."

I gladly let them.

They covered the incident tactfully and made the rest of the evening exceptionally enjoyable.

That night as I wheeled past my mirror I gave myself a quick glance. "Shut up farmer, and go to bed!"

Her mother left and we became very close. That week I got my car back from the shop.

She gave me one of her favorite books to read and we discussed it.

A woman was in love with a married man in wartime London. While they were cavorting, a German bomb struck the building and her lover was pinned and suffocating under a fallen timber. In desperation she promised God she would never see him again if He would grant him life. The building shifted, the timber moved off her lover and he lived. She loved him deeply, but her promise to God wouldn't let her see him again. The book followed her life as she traveled the world studying all religions trying to convince herself there was no God, so she could renege on her promise.

"What do you think of the story?" she asked.

"That's a tough one to answer. My few years in Catholic school influenced my life forever. Why? I can't answer. Songs we sang in the third grade give me wonderful feelings to sing now. And silly as it sounds. I can still feel myself holding a ribbon and running around the Maypole singing to The Virgin Mary, and I'll never forget the words."

"I wish I could believe like that." She said.

I wished I could help her, but I knew I wasn't knowledgeable enough so I decided to just be an interested listener. We talked deep into night. I was getting ready to leave when she asked. "How about going to a movie Friday night? There's one I especially want to see."

"Sure. Now that I got my car back, we can stop at Arnold's, grab some food and eat in the movie."

"No, not to a drive in. To a theater."

Again panic. "To—a—theater?"

"Sure, why not. It's a great movie and I've been to that theater before. It's accessible for wheelchairs."

"I—a—, who would go with us?"

"No one, silly. We'll go by ourselves."

I got a thought that would stop her. "Sounds good, but we have two chairs. I know you're strong, but you'd have to get one chair in the trunk."

"No problem," she answered. "Get Robert to take the back seat out of your car. That would give us enough room for both chairs."

Stuck for an answer, I hesitated.

"Come on Ray, it would be fun. Afraid of a challenge?"

She shamed me into agreeing to try. Robert removed the back seat. Friday night I opened the driver's door, locked my chair and slid on my board to the seat. I pulled the seat forward and Ann folded my chair and pushed it into the back seat. She whipped around the car, jumped in, folded her chair, pulled it in next to my chair and shut the door. "See how simple, let's go."

Robert watched in amazement and exclaimed, "Jesus, I couldn't do it that fast."

"Want to arm wrestle?" she challenged jokingly.

"No thanks. And Ray, you better not get too frisky with her."

I was laughing on the outside, but worrying on the inside. What if we get jammed in and can't get the doors open? What if there's a steep grade and I can't hack it? Without shoulder muscles I can't get the money up to the ticket window. If I go down the aisle, how will I get back up? What if the parking lot has holes or bumps I can't get over? She can pop a wheelie and jump up a curb. What if I gotta pee, or worse.

"You're awful quiet Ray. You haven't said a word since we left."

"Just thinking about how easily you did that."

"And, just a little apprehensive?"

"Naw," I lied. Then I looked at her and smiled. "You're getting to know me too well. Soon I won't have any secrets."

She laughed, then said, "here we are. Pull in the drive and back into the first spot next to the sidewalk. That way no one can block the driver's door."

"Smart ass," I thought. Then I tried to stump her. "What if someone blocks your side when we come out?"

"Then I'll get in your side, and drive away."

That was the last time I tried to stump her.

The walk was smooth, no incline, she bought the tickets, we got popcorn, sodas and found a good spot to park our chairs. In the middle of the movie I squeezed her hand, leaned over and whispered, "thanks."

She smiled and winked.

During the next weeks, I felt myself slowly gaining confidence in the outside world.

I thought I had learned it all until one Sunday morning. I was to meet her in the lobby at ten and we were going to drive down to San Diego for the day. I got off the elevator and she was talking to a tall good looking young man dressed in Navy whites. His hat was tucked neatly under his left arm and his right hand rested on the arm of her chair.

Their serious expressions caused me to wheel by and go to the lobby desk. I asked the receptionist, "would you talk to me please? I don't want to interfere with them."

"Sure." I was feeling uncomfortable myself. I think he's going to start crying."

"Really?"

The young officer was oblivious to the world. There was panic in his trembling voice. We tried not to hear his pleas, but his words were articulate, sad and loud. "But I love you." He said. "You are the world to me. Please marry me. I want to spend the rest of my life with you."

We couldn't hear Ann's answers.

Finally he said, "my life isn't worth living without you. I'll throw myself off the Santa Monica Pier."

Again we couldn't hear her response.

He bolted up straight, squared his shoulders, adjusted his hat with the brim exactly two fingers above his eyebrows. With toe to heel he spun around and marched out the open lobby door. We pretended our conversation kept us from seeing him leave.

Ann wheeled up and calmly said. "Ready to go Ray?"

We were a half hour down the coast before she said anything. "I'm sorry for the scene. I told him over the phone not to fly out. We dated when I was in college and he took our relationship too serious."

I thought of many things to say. Be serious, not serious, ignore it or change the subject. Change the subject, yes, best idea. But naturally I had to open my mouth. "Couldn't help hearing him say he was going to jump off the Pier? What did you say?"

"I told him jump, you're an excellent swimmer, just watch for sharks."

I learned a great lesson that day. A handsome able-bodied man that could have almost any girl he wanted was head over heels in love with a girl, confined for life, to a wheelchair. I looked at her with her red scarf blowing in the warm southern California wind. "Raymond," I said to myself. "She could be with that able bodied man. Yet she chose to be with you. Either she's nuts, or you have a lot to learn about this wonderful thing called, life."

The following week she asked if I would accompany her to a meeting.

"Sure," I answered. "What kind of a meeting?"

"You'll see," she answered mysteriously.

With a newspaper clipping in her hand we searched through the back streets of L.A.

"Wow!" I exclaimed as I scanned the desolate streets. "I wouldn't drive here in the daytime."

"It is spooky, but I was told the area is perfectly safe. If you're worried, we can leave."

"I'm not too worried as long as I have my automatic."

"You have a gun?"

"Absolutely."

"Do you have a permit?"

"No."

"What if you have to use it?"

"If my life is in jeopardy, I'd rather explain why I have it than be dead or hurt."

"I've always heard the bad guy can take your gun and use it against you."

"If your stupid enough to have a gun and don't know how and when to use it, you deserve what you get."

"Could you shoot someone?"

"Only if a life were in danger. Anyone can take my money, car or any material thing I own. Nothing like that is worth killing for. But if I saw the guys that were beating my friend with his own artificial legs, I would not hesitate."

"I suppose I could in that case."

"You can't suppose. You have to be sure and not hesitate. It is a horrible thought to take a life. I feel sorry for policemen. They have to say, 'stick 'em up.' Which is stupid. A friend taught me a valuable lesson. He gave me a gun without a cylinder, told me to cock the pistol, aim it at him and pull the trigger if he moved. He had a cowboy gun also with the cylinder removed in a holster on his hip. His hands were hanging at his side. He suddenly drew his pistol, cocked it and pulled the trigger before my reflex let me pull my trigger. His hammer struck the firing pin before mine did. We did it several times with the same results and I was expecting it. A professional doesn't hesitate, and you can't either."

"I don't know if I could handle that."

"Then don't carry a gun, and pray a lot."

"My father had a party. Some state legislatures were there and they were for gun control. Their argument was that the congress that drew up the fifth amendment couldn't dream how powerful weapons would be in this day and age."

"No!" I interrupted. "It isn't the powerful weapons they didn't figure on. They didn't figure on the men in Washington today. They are afraid to put teeth in the laws that are already on the books."

"Ray," she interrupted. "Put your spotlight on that storefront, yes, that's the address."

"Not many cars around and the place looks closed," I said hoping we might leave.

I parked, she jumped out, wheeled to the door and knocked. I held my automatic as I saw the door open. A large man listened to her as she pointed to the car. She waved as he walked around the car and lifted my chair out of the back seat. After I slid onto my chair, he got me up the curb and into the building. My 25 was in my corset. I was surprised as I counted nearly fifty people sitting on folding chairs. The speaker on the podium wore a white robe. It was some type of religious meeting. Though suspicious at first, I soon enjoyed his words. Weeks later, after assorted 'Cult' meetings, Ann finally asked. "What do you think?"

"Well, I felt guilty at first. My religion says not to attend other churches, which I disagree with. My church celebrates the Mass in Latin. I only went to the fifth grade in Catholic school and I'm ashamed to say I really don't understand the Mass. These meetings were in English and I thoroughly enjoyed the speakers. I wish our priests would say the Mass in English, but Catholics will be allowed to eat meat on Friday before that'll ever happen."

"I appreciate your candidness Ray. I've studied many religions, but for every door I opened, I found two behind it. This is the last meeting for me and thanks for your patience and company."

"Ann, I have an unusual outlook on religion, so please don't think less of Catholicism because of any views I may have."

"I promise, go ahead."

"I believe religion is pure common sense. Obeying the Commandments is logical if you want a happy and safe life. If you injure or kill someone, you go to jail. If you mess with another's spouse, you can get shot. If you covet another's property and steal it, you can go to jail.

Some smart people way back figured it out, but knew they couldn't just tell people what was good for them. Man still has the kill or be killed genes from caveman days. So they wrote many examples [Scriptures] to drill logical answers into our hard heads.

An example: Speed Limit signs."

Ann laughed and raised her eyebrows. "Speed Limit Signs?"

"Sure, think about it. Do you need them now? Or do you drive according to conditions? If a sign says sixty-five and the roads are slippery, do you drive sixty-five?"

"No."

"But I bet you did when you first started driving."

"Yes," she admitted.

"See, as you matured, you learned you can hurt or be hurt by not being careful. You needed the signs at first to keep you alive long enough to learn. The same with religion. You need it desperately when you start life. You need the moral teachings burned into your very being. Of course, some ignore learning. Jails and cemeteries are full of them."

"So your saying mature adults don't need Speed Limit signs or religion?"

"Mature and adult do no always go together. I believe you keep needing religion for your own well being, but most important for the example you set for your children."

"You make it sound simple."

"It is simple, if you want it to be. Maybe I understand because I have a simple mind."

"So you're simple-minded, Ray?"

"I guess if the shoe fits."

Just then a car pulled out of a side street and I hit the brakes barely missing it. Ann nearly slid off the seat. She had to reach in the back seat to readjust our chairs.

"Are you okay?" I asked.

"Yes, but I thought we had it."

"I'm glad I saw him in time."

"I have a question to ask. I've noticed that when someone cuts you off or pulls out in front of you, you don't yell or swear at them. How can you do it?"

"Here I go again. It's simple to me. I've made plenty of mistakes. I always look both ways at least twice before I pull out into traffic. Still, cars have swerved to miss me. They appeared like magic. They must have been behind a pole, tree or sign each time I looked. I try to drive carefully, but I have inadvertently cut cars off. So, I figure if I've made that mistake, how can I yell at someone else."

"That's more control than I have. What about the jerk that sees you coming and cuts you off anyway?"

"Oh, I get hot automatically, but again I give them the benefit of the doubt. I'd rather think he made a mistake. Yelling and getting myself upset doesn't help, and I feel better afterwards."

We were on the Sunset Strip and came to Hollywood and Vine. I stopped the car in the middle of the intersection.

"What are you doing?" she asked looking at the traffic.

"I've always wanted to kiss a girl at Hollywood and Vine."

I pulled her over and kissed her, then drove away.

She studied me for a moment then smiled. "I liked that. My common sense thought it was a little bazaar, but my heart thought it was very sweet."

I smiled to myself as she rested her head on my shoulder for the drive back to Santa Monica.

She left the institute several weeks later. I learned much from her. Most important, she taught me to be comfortable in the 'outside world.'

Several weeks later, Amie's best Jill was admitted to CRC. She was an Olympic hopeful that broke her neck in a skiing accident. She was strikingly beautiful. What a twist of fate. Amie got Polio, and Kim drove her around. Then Kim became paralyzed and Amie was there for her.

Then *my* time to leave arrived. After eighteen months and a lifetime of wonderful experiences, I was leaving my nest.

I did not want to leave. I wanted to stay there forever. I was ready for the outside world, but apprehension gnawed at my optimism.

CHAPTER SIX

THE BREAKS

As my brother and I crossed the sweltering Mojave Desert heading East, I had mixed feelings. Although I missed my, family, and home for the last eighteen months, I knew I had to get on with my life. I stored my treasury of grand memories and looked forward to returning home. When I left Ohio, I was *completely* dependent, now, I didn't have to ask—to be dressed, helped to sit up in my chair, washed, shaved or fed. I could go to the john when *I* wanted to, or go for a drive when I felt like it. I could also come home, get undressed and go to bed without being an inconvenience to anyone. My progress in eighteen months was truly miraculous.

On the way we stopped at a hotel in Kansas City. At ten that evening a gorgeous brunette knocked at our door, offering herself for a fee. My brother asked if I was interested. I was far from everyone, except myself. That's the funny thing about saving yourself for twenty-odd years. You hate to lose that one thing that makes you feel different. I fell asleep in the middle of my prayers.

A week later we drove into our farm. Things felt wonderfully different as I wheeled up the small ramp into our home. After my mother, I was most happy to see Marilyn. Her shy smile hadn't changed a bit. The next morning I picked her up and we drove through the nursery with the top down.

"Remember the first time I drove us across the street to the pond?"

"Yes, in your homemade golf cart. I was thrilled. I didn't think you wanted to spend time with a kid like me. While you were in California, I worried you would come home married."

Not understanding my feelings yet, I changed the subject. "How about you and Jack?"

"He doesn't like the idea that you're home."

"I can't blame him. He had you all to himself for a long time. Did you have time to think about me?"

"I thought about you all the time. Did you think about me, or were you too busy with those California girls?"

I didn't want to lie, yet I didn't want to hurt her either, so again I changed directions.

"Tell me about Jack. How serious is he?"

"He talked marriage and would become angry when I avoided the subject. He insisted you would forget me when you returned and that you were only using me. He wouldn't believe we didn't have sex."

"I can hardly believe it myself. You are a very attractive sexy woman. Are you sure he didn't catch you in a weak moment?"

"No!" She answered indignantly with a look of disbelief that I would even think that.

I've heard a lot of stories from a fair amount of girls and Marilyn is the only one I believed completely. We laughed and hugged then went to a drive-in for a cup of coffee. She never pressed marriage. I felt a terrific responsibility for her life, and I was not yet sure of my feelings. My life just changed dramatically and I was trying to find myself. I worried that if I started her on sex and then did not marry her, I would do her a great injustice. I knew her feelings for me made her vulnerable.

I was obsessed to be active in the nursery. I had a ramp built to a platform so my chair was level with a Cub Tractor seat. I used my sliding board to transfer to the seat and with a hand clutch I would cultivate.

The sun and exercise made me feel great, but more important, useful.

My brother was divorced and lived with Mom and me. It was a wonderful summer. I wouldn't go out with girls I dated pre polio because I was afraid of being pitied. My theory was, a new acquaintance could turn me down without guilt. I dated some local college girls. And, Ann surprised me with a visit. Marilyn, who lived next door knew every time I went out. It hurt me deeply to see her unhappy. I prayed I was doing the right thing.

The Cleveland hospital, where I spent the first ten months, sent me an invitation to a picnic. I remembered an ex-patient I met during those first dark months. His improvements helped me think there *might* be hope for me. I put on my turquoise sweater that matched my car, and with the top down I drove to the old Toomey Pavilion.

It was an exceptionally beautiful summer day. The hospital had a half dozen long tables set up under the canopy of several ancient maples. About twenty-five patients and some family members were there.

It did feel spooky. The painful memory of my long months in an iron lung tore at my senses. I could smell and feel the steaming, itchy, wool hot-packs. I remembered the endless pain of stretching and the hopeless months when I couldn't move my arms enough to scratch my nose. I pictured myself, five years earlier, walking into the hospital for a check up. I felt like crying as I looked at the decaying old

Isolation Division, but the patient's joy seeing someone that was devastated by Polio, able to drive again pushed the painful thoughts from of my mind. Near the end of the meal, I asked a nurse to get a bag from under my car seat. She was a good sport and on her hands and knees crawled under the tables pouring a bit of whiskey in each patient's soft drink. Before long, the bottle was empty and everyone was singing. I felt good knowing that for a short time, in their long ordeal, they felt happy and carefree. It was a wonderful day for me.

Euphoria swept me through a wonderful summer. My brother built standing bars, and with one brace I would walk every day.

Mom bought a house in Ft. Lauderdale and after Thanksgiving we drove south. Grandma rode with Mom, and I led driving my car. It was an exciting trip trying not to lose her in thirteen hundred miles of driving through dozens of small towns. There were no super highways at that time.

Marilyn and her parents drove to Lauderdale for the holidays. Her parents stayed with relatives and Marilyn stayed with us. One day my mother and grandmother left for a day of shopping. We decided to act grown up and took a shower together. She helped me onto the tile bench and we were having a lathering time. Naturally my mother forgot something and returned home. Marilyn dressed quickly, but I couldn't explain what I was doing in the shower. The only thing she said to me was, "don't do anything to ruin your lives." We didn't.

After Marilyn left, I was more confused than ever. Did I want to get married now? I knew in my heart Marilyn and I were meant for each other, but the drive to experience my new life was overwhelming…

After Marilyn left my cousin, Charley came down from Ohio to spend some time with us. I was glad to have someone I could travel around with. A few weeks after Marilyn left, Charley and I went bar hopping. About midnight we found a new bar.

"There's a bar called, The Velvet Cat, let's try it."

"Okay, sounds interesting but there's several steps, want to try em?"

"Sure, takes more than steps to stop us." How prophetic that statement turned out to be.

I parked and he easily pulled me up the steps. The music was slow and sultry. A girl was dancing on one of the tables until she fell off. Luckily her boyfriend caught her.

"How did we miss this place?"

"I don't know, Ray. There are a lot of good-looking women here."

A waitress with a very short dress lit our cigarettes and took our order. We were on our second round when Charley got a smile from a girl sitting at the bar. So he went over and asked her to dance. They did and after the song he returned to the table with her friend.

The second girl asked, "what are two good-looking guys like you doing out by your selves?"

I answered, "I was just going to ask you the same thing."

Charley and the other girl danced, while Darlene and I talked.

I can't remember what all we talked about, but she was soon leaning on my chair with her hand on my thigh. It thrilled and scared me at the same time. She was voluptuous. Her short red hair contrasted with a long pair of pearl earrings. I was thinking about her beauty when she said. "Ray, I have never met anyone like you before."

I almost answered, "you mean a gimp?" But I didn't.

"I bet you tell that to all the six-foot six guys you meet."

"No," she answered seriously. "I'm not joking. I mean it. I'd like to take you home tonight."

I felt a lightning bolt nearly lift me out of my chair. She continued. "The things we talked about for the last two hours were not just idle chatter. I've been *studying* you."

"Studying me, I don't understand."

"For one thing, you're a virgin, aren't you?"

"God. Is it that obvious?"

"To me it is. It's the way you talk, with respect. I'm not used to that, and it feels good."

She looked down and fixed her attention to the flowered pattern on the red table clothe.

"I can't take you to my apartment tonight. I'm leaving in an hour for the weekend. A very rich foreign playboy is picking up twenty girls tonight for a weekend on his yachet, and I am one of them." After an awkward hesitation she lifted her head slowly and looked at me. I felt she was looking into my soul. "I can't believe I told you that."

"I'm glad you did." Was all I could think to say.

She smiled, "I knew you'd say that."

"Another test?"

Still smiling, and rested her warm hand on mine.

"I'm not drunk or high, and I'm going to tell you something very private." Her eyes never left my face.

"I'm twenty-three and I have a six-year-old beautiful girl. She lives with my sister and goes to a private school. She is the most important thing in my life. The time we spend together is the only bright side of my life." Then her smile disappeared and her hand gently squeezed mine. "I have a *lot* of money put away in a dozen banks. My parents are dead and I'm worried about my daughter."

I felt I had to say something.

"Is your sister married?"

"That's the problem. She's married to a bum. She works and he lives off her. I give them money for my girl and the asshole gets a new car. I give more money and he comes up with a motorcycle."

I shook my head. "And I bet your sister is beautiful."

"Why do you say that?"

"The pattern in this crazy world is a beautiful young girl gets sexually involved with an older jerk. The nice guys her age are boring because they are courteous and caring. And once she starts, she's addicted."

"Damn, Ray, you're exactly right. How did you know—?"

"Not all guys that know girls' weaknesses take advantage of them."

"I wish I'd have met one, before."

Her sentence dropped off. I didn't want to hurt her feelings, so I didn't say, "they were there, but they were the boring ones."

Then she became very serious. "Yesterday is yesterday. Tomorrow is the important thing, and I am worried. Girl's I work with are disappearing."

"Disappearing?"

"Yes. I'm not saying it is or isn't foul play. It could be with a john, or they go to foreign countries, or diseases or just quit. But I never hear from a lot of them. And many of my friends are winding up in hospitals. I worry what will happen to my girl if something happens to me."

I began to wonder what I was getting involved in. The picture in my mind of this beautiful girl pleasing a bunch of fat old fart's sickened me, but at the same time intrigued me.

"I'll be here Monday night. I really want to talk to you again, if you're interested."

"We'll be here," I answered automatically.

Her friend looked at her watch. "I hate to interrupt but its time to go."

Darlene handed me a paper. "Here is my phone number, please call me." She leaned over, kissed me on the cheek and left.

Charley looked at me. "What were you two talking about all evening? She didn't know anyone else was in the joint."

"She wants to meet us here Monday night."

"Great, they're knockouts."

While Charley danced with another girl, many questions raced through my mind. "Do you know what you're getting involved in, Ray? If you wind up in her apartment and change your mind it won't work like the past, know it now."

Charley interrupted my thoughts, "Ray, I got a girl that wants to party all night. She can get a friend—"

"No thanks, Charley, you go play. I have a lot to think about and I'm tired. Do you want the car?"

"No, she's got wheels, are you sure you don't want her to get her friend?"

"No, just get me down the steps. I'll be all right."

I drove to the pier where fishing boats are berthed. The flood lights swayed from the ocean breezes casting dancing shadows on the empty racks where the day's catches are displayed. The dark fishing vessels rocked gently, resting for their next day's work. It was peaceful. I lit a Lucky, looked up at the heavens and said. "Thanks Boss."

Then I glanced at my right shoulder and smiled. "Pops, I wish you could be here. You and Mom are the ones that made everything possible. How lucky I was there was enough money to send me to California. Without that, I shudder to think where I'd be. I'm sure it wouldn't be here.

I have a dilemma, Pops. Do I show up Monday night? "I remember you telling me about the girls you used to go out with. They would grab you and ask if it was alive. How did you know, so accurately, when I would be facing a new challenge? Your stories about driving, drinking and living were all followed by my running into that particular situation. You helped me through so many things."

Tears welled up in my eyes. "God I miss you so much, don't ever leave my shoulder."

I drove home slowly wanting to enjoy every second of the warm

Gulf stream breezes. I backed into our garage, got into my chair and wheeled into the family room.

Out of the shadows I heard my mother ask, "Where's Charley?"

"He met a girl."

"It's after three."

"Mother," I said indignantly. "I'm twenty-five years old."

"I know. I wasn't waiting up for you. I just went to the bathroom, then heard a siren. It got me nervous and I was just sitting here."

"Mother. There are thousands of cars out there."

"I know," she interrupted. "It's just being a parent, wait until you're one."

Wow, how right she was.

Two days later, Sunday morning, Charily and I went to Mass. It was a usual south Florida day.

As we left the church, we saw a priest acknowledging the departing parishioners. Charley and I looked at him and nodded. The next thing I knew my face was sideways, smashed against the sidewalk. My eyes focused on my broken glasses as I tried to understand what happened. Several men helped Charley lift me back into my chair. The beautiful sunny day turned into a nightmare.

I heard panic in Charley's voice. "Oh God, Ray, what did I do? Are you all right?"

I tried to shake the cobwebs out of my head hoping it was just a bad dream, but the pain I felt in both knees told me it wasn't

I thought, "Raymond, you really did it this time. You know you have to be on guard every second." I looked back and saw the four-inch step we didn't see. Charlie and I were both looking at the priest and missed seeing it.

My front wheels dropped off and my pedals hit the concrete. The chair stopped and I slid out. My knees and face hit, but worst, I sat back on my heels. My body weight bent my tight knees beyond their range of motion. The intense pain kept me from getting into the car and driving to a hospital. Luckily a parishioner had a pickup truck. Several men lifted my chair onto the bed of the truck and drove me to a brand-new hospital that just opened. The new staff was mixed up. I sat for two hours before anyone realized I was waiting for x-rays. Finally a nurse gave me a shot for pain and got me to x-ray. The shot didn't have time to help much as they lifted me onto the table and took pictures of my knees. The results came back. Both knees were fractured. The shot finally took effect and the next thing I knew I was in the operating room being prepared for casts. I remember the doctor asking if my legs were ever straight. My answer must have confused them and they cast them bent. Bad move! I stupidly thought that it would be easy to stretch a little to straighten them and a little to bend them, wrong! It turned out to be one of the biggest mistakes of my life.

My mother was extremely unhappy with my cousin and my cousin blamed himself. He was beside himself with guilt.

"No, Charley," I said. "It is not your fault. I know better. I have trained myself to be aware of everything and not to relax for a second. I am always vulnerable, like wheeling on the edge of Grand Canyon. One mistake, and a catastrophe.

You are not used to that so don't blame yourself. We went up and down stairs in a dozen bars, while drinking, with no problems. Being sober and going to Church was our mistake."

That got a little smile from him, but he never did forgive himself.

After everyone left and my pain shot was taking effect, I studied my two long casts. "Gee Pops, if you didn't want me to meet that girl at the Velvet Cat, you could have given me a little less dramatic sign."

After four months in the casts I flew home on a stretcher. My poor mother was in tears most of the time.

On the flight, I severely chastised myself. "You've done it again, Ray. Another knife in Mom's heart."

It was snowing lightly at Cleveland Hopkins when we landed. On the thirty-mile ambulance ride home I looked out the window at the barren trees. This time my homecoming was very different. My heart ached, but I made up my mind no one would know how much.

Six months in a bent position and six more months of limited exercise deformed my hips and knee joints eliminating my ability to use standing bars. Without those exercises, it was the beginning of the end of my progress. I debated returning to California for months of treatment, but the uncertainty of the results, cost, and more time out of my life didn't seem a worthwhile option. I starved to get on with my life.

The long days and nights spent in my confining casts made me face my disability and life. I knew I'd get well enough to play around socially again and I truly enjoyed women. Their different personalities, beliefs, traits and laughs were wonderful things. Some of my friends asked what I saw in Marilyn. She was quiet, shy and not worldly. I knew all those things, but she had the greatest, purest devoted heart I had ever encountered. I still can't figure how I was perceptive enough to figure that out. Picking her for a lifetime mate was the only perfect decision I ever made, if it was my decision. I am convinced God created us to be mates.

I remembered three years earlier at the beginning of our relationship, while Marilyn was visiting I had to use the bed pan. My mother asked her to empty it. My sister was there and we were both furious with our mother.

"How could you embarrass me like that?" I asked.

My sister added, "Ray is just getting to know her, you shouldn't have done that."

My mother's retort, "If she has any interest in Raymond, she might as well know what a life with him involves."

Forty years later, I marvel at the foresight of a woman that never attended school in America.

All these thoughts were tumbling through my mind as I regained my ability to function independently again. I decided not to waste another moment of my life chasing unimportant things, and proposed marriage to Marilyn. To my joy she accepted.

At this time my mother was being nagged by a sore back and she went to the hospital. They found cancer in her pelvic, and a cloud of doom formed over our home.

A week later the "cloud of doom" grew. She fell getting out of the hospital bed and her cancer weakened femur shattered and it couldn't be repaired. They amputated the leg and removed part of her hip. The doctor's prognosis, one year to live.

Despite the Grim Reaper poised to swing his lethal scythe, Mother insisted on handling the plans for our marriage. Marilyn's parents were apprehensive and questioned her many times. I could well understand their misgivings. Marilyn was always timid with her parents, but where I was concerned she was the Rock of Gibraltar.

We were married June 28, 1958. We honeymooned in Ft. Lauderdale and had a wonderful three weeks.

Mother converted an end of the house for Marilyn and me. Mothers' determination and strong heart kept her alive more than three years. One would think that extra time was a blessing, but in truth she spent her last two years in agony praying to die.

Marilyn's love of people showed from the start. She bathed, massaged, cooked, cleaned, and gave Mom her shots besides being my arms and legs. Injections of morphine every four hours quelled her pain at first. By the last six months, every fifteen minutes failed to ease her tortuous, constant pain. Every day, every night, all night her muffled cries of agony echoed throughout the house.

My complete love of God and belief in His wisdom carried me through my own tribulations, but all my understanding died watching my mother's torment. Dying I could understand, but to be tortured to death was way beyond my comprehension.

I would scream to the heavens. "How can You allow this to happen to a woman that never did anything wrong? A woman that sacrificed every personal need for her family!"

My faith died a thousand times in those years.

The day before she passed away, she held Marilyn's hand and in a weak voice whispered to her, "I can die happy now, knowing Raymond is in good hands."

At the cemetery with Marilyn, under a tent with my brother, sister, family and friends we listened to the priest's prayers. Marilyn's hand was on my shoulder as I studied the headstone.

Joseph P. Youdath. Born 1896. Died 1948.
Mary F. Youdath. Born 1900. Died 1959.

As the priest spoke, my thoughts were of my father.

"Dad, you were only fifty-two, and Mother a young fifty-nine. The years when you could finally enjoy the fruits of your unselfish sacrifices and enjoy your grandchildren were ripped from you without mercy. I feel so bad for you, and for me. I have so much to learn and God took my two most trusted teachers. I will try not to be bitter, but his (My eyes focused on the priest's mouth speaking.) words are empty."

Our first child, Debbie, was born in November. Two months after my mother died. She tried to live long enough to see our baby, but even that was taken from her.

Years passed as we all tried to put our lives back on track.

In 1959 we purchased a Pontiac station wagon and discovered it had extraordinary pickup. Some friends suggested I race it at a local drag strip. I didn't expect it to do well, but we went to the track and signed in. A friend was in the bleachers when my white wagon pulled up to the line next to a new Ford coupe.

A girl sitting in front of my friend commented about my car. Her boyfriend answered, "That heavy wagon doesn't have a chance."

The flag-man jumped and waved the start flag. My wagon leaped ahead by several car-lengths and won easily.

I was more surprised than anyone. There were a dozen cars in my class and I beat them all winning a beautiful trophy. Needless to say, I was hooked. I finally found a sport in which I could compete. I won more than forty trophies in the next two years.

Our new partner in the nursery, Dan, constantly ribbed me.

"How do you have time for kid games?" he jibbed.

"Dan," I tried to explain, "I can't golf or—"

"GOLF!" he interrupted. "How can anyone waste time hitting a little white ball, then chase it all over the place? Anyone that does that is still playing with themselves. For Christ sake, Ray, have you got all the money you need? Do you have any idea how much you're gonna need to raise three brats?"

"But Dan, you played pool, had speed boats, flew your own plane and you get the first new green Cadillac every year."

"Boy, you are dense. I played pool to beat suckers out of their money. I had a Garwood speed boat to haul whiskey from Canada to Cleveland. I did the same with the plane. I'd land in back of our farm. It was all to make money."

"What about the Cadillacs?" I asked.

"I don't give a damn about the car, but when I took a customer into the nursery to sell him a block of trees in a brand-new Caddy, it took the chisel out of the mope. "The first block of plants paid for the car. The extra thirty or forty G's for other blocks went into my piggy bank. Anyone can make a million dollars. All they gotta do is work. Now remember what I say. No one has more than twenty-four hours a day. Not Rockefeller, Ford, Flagler, you or me. What counts is what you do with the twenty-four hours. You can study and make money, or you can play silly games."

Then his lip curled causing his right cheek to raise and his eye squinted.

I hated that smirk. It made me feel like I was treated to a revelation by Einstein himself.

He ended his lesson. "Be careful driving home. You look confused."

In retrospect, most of his words, though painful, were accurate. I realized the tougher the lesson, the better it's remembered. And I admit I did fool myself. Losing my ability to walk should not have given me the excuse to waste precious time.

The sermon in church the next Sunday drove the point home.

The priest started with a question. "What do you think God will say to you when you face him for final judgment? He won't look at a record book and say, you missed Mass six hundred and twenty two times, you swore three thousand four hundred and twelve times, ate meat on Fridays five-hundred times. No! That is not what He will ask you. What He *will* ask is: What did you do with the precious time I gave you on earth? What did you do with your life?"

Those words burned deep and were never forgotten.

A killing frost in June lost us a year of saleable plants. I had to look for a job. A patient I met in Warm Springs worked at the Plain Dealer newspaper. He arranged an interview and I got a job in the circulation department. Though the pay at the newspaper was minimal to start, I finally felt useful. I was allowed to use my creative brain. I was like a child turned loose in a candy store. I tried to revolutionize everything. One day I went into the director's office to complain about a problem I found. We were interrupted by a supervisor who complained about a problem he encountered. After he left the director shook his head. "Everybody comes in with a complaint, but never a solution."

I thought Oh-o. The director asked what I wanted. "I just wanted to say good morning," I answered and exited quickly. I was going to present a problem without a solution.

The Circulation Dept. was blamed for everything. I began keeping detailed records and a few weeks later went into the director's office armed with facts, figures and a solution. He checked with several department heads and found my figures unquestionable and implemented my program.

The other departments weren't happy with the extra work, but the sixty-odd workers in my department felt vindicated from past accusations. In the following years I implemented a half dozen new programs.

The lean years in the nursery limited vacations. Then the fringe benefits of working for a great newspaper kicked in. To increase circulation the Contest Department promoted many trips for the paperboys and girls. Chaperons were needed for the scores of carriers that won the trips.

It was a true blessing for my vacation starved family.

Marilyn, Debbie, David, John and I enjoyed vacations at Cedar Point, Kings Island, Expo 67 in Canada, resorts and scores of plays. One vacation that I'll always remember was a trip to Niagara Falls. While there, we heard of a great restaurant overlooking Horseshoe Falls.

The five of us looked forward to a great treat. We dressed and headed for the eatery. When we got there, we found the only entrance was up a flight of twenty steps.

I saw the disappointed look on their faces.

Debbie spoke first. "Oh well, we can find another place to eat." The rest of the family agreed and started to walk away.

"Wait a minute, guys, are we a team or what?"

Puzzled, Marilyn asked, "what do you mean?"

"There are four of you. Marilyn, take one handle and David the other. Tip me back and pull me up the steps. Debbie, you hold one pedal and John, you hold the other. If Mom or Dave slips, you guys can keep the chair tipped back."

"Dad, are you sure you want to take the chance?" Debbie asked.

"Hey, we are a team and we can do anything we put our minds to. "I said with the most confidence I could muster as I looked up the mountain of steps.

They tipped me back and I called cadences. "One step at a time and all together." We started up. I am used to being looked at and I saw a dozen people watching us.

"We have an audience, gang. Let's give 'em a good show."

My heart was bursting with pride for my family when we got to the top.

As we turned and started to wheel to the frond doors, we heard clapping from the group of on lookers. Our three children each grew a foot taller that day.

CHAPTER SEVEN

WILD RIDE

Marilyn had an unhappy childhood. Her father was an alcoholic and her mother denied his addiction to the outside world, but inside the house she would scream and kick him when he would fall. He suffered a few cracked ribs. Marilyn and her sister never experienced closeness with their parents. After we married, it took years before Marilyn could hug and show affection. Her sister married early to leave the environment.

Conflicts in my house caused me to contact Catholic charities and they set us up with a councilor. The psychologist, Mrs. Orton was wonderful. She soon learned Marilyn believed if she gave complete love and care to her children, they would automatically be humble loving children. Her heart was broken a thousand times and she shed a pool full of tears.

After a dozen visits, Mrs. Orton asked to see me alone. In her office she surprised me and said, "Ray, let's talk about you."

"Me?"

"Yes. How are *you* doing?"

"I'm doing okay. Why, did I say something wrong in our meetings?"

"On the contrary, your insight is in line with my thoughts."

"Then why?"

"My question is why do you belittle yourself so much?"

I answered automatically. "Truthfully, what can I say about myself that's good?"

"How can you say that?"

"Easy, just look at the things you've learned since we started. I've failed as a husband and father."

"Raymond, you and, Marilyn have done a great job. When I talk to your children, they show love and respect."

"They do?"

"Yes, and if you think they are unruly, you have not seen unruly, believe me. Yours are normal healthy children that will grow to fine adults. My concern is you. Again I ask, why do you belittle yourself so much?"

I must have looked puzzled as my mind flooded with painful instances. "Relax and say what you feel."

I felt secure with her, and words poured out from hidden places.

"Mrs. Orton, I have felt *kept* since I got Polio. After I woke up from my weeks in a coma, I began to comprehend my shattered world. My optimism was severely wounded as I realized that I would never walk again, and probably live the rest of my life in an Iron Lung. I had to mentally avoid those facts and retreated to my imagination, allowing me to escaped to wonderful adventures and romantic places. I learned quickly that if a patient demanded service, complained or cried about their illness, they were avoided. I remember the first day I was put on a Gurney and pushed outside on the balcony. It was a beautiful Sunday in July. The warm smell of summer stirred my memories. The nurse's quarters were across the street, and I watched a string of cars pull in. The boys would get their dates and leave for the beach or picnics. I pictured myself and my new Ford convertible with the top down picking up a beautiful young girl. Then the realization that my new car was sold, and my wonderful world was gone, caused so much pain I asked to be taken back to my room. Too much sun was my excuse."

I stared silently at the floor remembering the pain. A few moments later I looked at Mrs. Orton. She smiled and I continued. "After nine months in City Hospital I miraculously escaped the Iron Lung and was flown to Warm Springs, Ga. Franklin D. Roosevelt's winter home that he donated to the Polio foundation. They 'Jerry rigged' an antique wooden wheelchair to accommodate my tall frame. I was perched on a box, a tall skeleton with arms dangling in slings so I could feed myself. The girls considered me less than nothing. Boys able to wheel themselves went to all the parties and got the girls. This was a new and heartbreaking experience. My therapy consisted of stretching, which I can only describe as torture. After ten months of immobility my muscles had all shortened and atrophied. People in the eighteenth century that were tortured on, The Rack, had nothing on me. When stretched, my muscles felt like red-hot claws were ripping them to shreds. I actually couldn't eat supper knowing what the next day would bring. One day in the pool, while on my stomach, my red headed therapist was stretching my back. The pain was so intense, I dropped my head off the headrest into the water knowing she would have to stop and lift it out. I was prepared to drown rather than continue the pain.

After a few months at Warm Springs the doctors said there was nothing more they could do for me, and sent me home. The blazing torch of confidence that once consumed me was down to a flicker."

I looked down at the floor while tears created a pattern on my trousers.

Mrs. Orton handed me a glass of water and a box of Kleenex. "Take your time, Ray. Continue when you feel able."

My throat welcomed the cool water. I smiled a thank you, and continued. "I hope I'm not jumping around too much."

"Jump wherever you want."

"One day I was riding around the nursery in my home made golf cart and saw one of our men working on a tractor. He was cursing because the blades on the disc were frozen. I suggested changing the grease fitting. He did and put fresh grease in solving the problem. He thanked me and went back to the field. It was an insignificant thing, but for the first time in three years I felt useful.

Then I went to a hospital in California and with the help of a fantastic therapist I improved more than I dreamed possible. When I returned home, I rigged a hand control on a Cub tractor and spent hours in the fields cultivating. I was slowly beginning to feel useful and my flame of confidence grew a bit from a flicker.

Then, enter Dan. An ex-gambler, racketeer, rum runner and God only knows what else. He quit the rackets, he said, and became a successful Nurseryman. He was fascinating and likable, and a legend in his own time. He became our partner and in two whirlwind years transformed our haphazard nursery into a potential big business, but his way of teaching was unmerciful. What he said was logical, but cut very deep.

Example: "You should have been twins, you're too dumb for one person. How can you find your way home at night? My father gave me forty-eight postcards and told me to send him one from every state and I did. That's what you mopes need. Ride in boxcars with a wife and baby. Beg food from poor blacks in Georgia. Take a chance of getting killed while running a crooked card game in the oil fields in

Texas, so you can feed your kid. You're both spoiled."

My dad died when I was seventeen. My condition must have made me desperate for a father figure, so I accepted his chastising. He and my brother ran everything. It made me feel lucky to be along for the ride. I begged to be given responsibility. Let me be in charge of bedding plants, field planting, equipment, spraying or weed control, then yell at me if my job isn't done.

But all they told me,was balance the checkbook and pick up the help. My brother's second wife didn't like Dan and wanted him out of the nursery. Again, I found myself the middle and my head felt like it was in a vice. Dan felt cheated and his words scared me but not my brother. I guess I was naive or stupid, but I was afraid my brother might be hurt. I felt an obligation to both parties and suggested a plan. They were both unhappy. I wondered why was I always committed to morality. Then, a hard frost in June killed a years growth on two hundred thousand plants that needed to be maintained for a year without income. I was elected to find an outside job. I hated to ask for favors because I knew the results would be negative and they were. Which again proved my worthlessness. At a Polio picnic I met a boy I had befriended at Warm Springs. He worked at the Plain Dealer and told me to apply for an opening. I did and was hired. Six days a week, five a.m. to eleven-thirty for ninety dollars a week, and lucky to get it. What proved to be the biggest blessing was I got hospitalization.

I would rush home to the nursery to help. I drove around the hundred acres and traveled the dirt roadways that a few years earlier saw me flying around on one of our tractors.

One day, while feeling melancholy, I parked in the hay field remembering the blistering heat of the August sun as I loaded the hay wagon. My mind pictured the cloud of hay dust that would stick to my sweating body.

God, how I longed to feel it again. Then as I looked at a block of Junipers next to the hay field.

My mind pictured two Hungarian women in their long grey dresses, hoeing in the summer heat. I saw myself running to them with a jug of iced Cool Aid. I loved them dearly and I'd stop at the ice cream store after work when taking them home. The smile on their weathered faces under their bonnets when I handed them their nightly cone warmed my heart. Then I pictured Dad with his small brimmed, black hat, red knitted sleeveless sweater smoking his corncob pipe. Then after my trip back in time I drove home drying my tears wondering why Dad had to die so young. I felt hopelessly lost without him.

At this time the land was in my bother, sister and my name. No one agreed on how to divide it. Another disagreement. They wouldn't argue with each other, but they would vent their disapprovals to me.

I worked hard to get my brother the section with buildings, greenhouses and irrigation well. I knew it would be impossible for him to buy all the things needed to start a nursery elsewhere. My brother-in-law wanted to sell all the property and divide the money, but at that time the property wasn't worth much.

The ninety-dollars a week was barely enough to exist. My mother-in-law worked in a school cafeteria and saved us much on food. We never bought new furniture and the kids wore hand-me-downs and second hand clothes. The only vacations we took were with the Plain Dealer.

I needed exercise badly and two friends from work hand dug a base and set up an above-the-ground pool. It cost five hundred very scarce dollars. My wife asked why I didn't ask the family for help. Again, my unworthy feeling stopped me.

I felt I was a liability to everyone except my wife, children and black Terrier, Mitzi. They were the only ones in the world that loved me unconditionally."

I stopped again knowing I was beyond my allotted time. Mrs. Orton sensed what I was thinking. "Raymond, I know this is extremely painful, if you want to stop, feel free to do so, but you are my last client and I have plenty of time if you wish to continue."

She leaned back. Her short red hair was complimented by her green leather chair. Her smile encouraged me to continue.

"When the inheritance tax came, we found that our lawyer forgot to file papers on time and the tax was fifty four-thousand dollars. One third was no problem for my brother or sister. I panicked not knowing what to do. I knew the land was my future and if I sold it then, my future was doomed. My brother said he would pay my eighteen thousand dollar inheritance taxes for my half of the nursery. I hated to sell knowing it was worth twice that amount, but I had no choice and I felt I never contributed anything anyway. I'd been carried since I was nineteen. I'd been ridiculed by Dan until I thought my head would explode. I finally told him to just tell me straight out what he thought." He answered. "In the rackets you learn to talk a lot, but say nothing anyone can quote. That lesson cost me all my teeth except for two. They left those so I'd never forget. I'm trying to teach you so you'll never forget."

I paused in my story, took a drink of water and looked at Mrs. Orton. "Well, that's about it to the present."

She carefully leafed through her notes and looked up. "Is that all?"

I sensed a question. "Are you asking about something in particular?"

"Yes, I feel you're holding back about family matters."

"You're right, there is a lot more, but I am afraid to talk about it. I'm not sure how to look at family things. You told my wife that nobody can make you angry, except yourself. I have chosen not get angry even if I feel wronged. I'm sure all people feel they are right in what they do, so who am I to say who is right and who is wrong. Even if I could prove someone wrong, I'm afraid of what it would do to me inside. Maybe I *am* a mouse."

"Raymond, you just touched on many chapters of advanced psychology. You've come up with answers we try to teach. The bottom line is being happy with yourself, and I think you are doing a great job."

I smiled with puzzlement. I said what I felt, not knowing if it really made much sense.

She continued, "I have pages of monumental obstacles you have overcome in spite of your disability. You should be very proud of yourself, Raymond. You have held your family together." My only answer was. "I could never have done anything without Marilyn."

I never told anyone about our conversation. Until then, I thought common sense would keep one on track. She taught me any mind could be subtly corrupted. The important lesson *was. Never think you cannot learn about yourself.* My admiration toward psychologists grew. She opened a window to my inner-self that was always there to open, but for that wonderful lady it would still be shut tight.

After our meeting she invited Marilyn and me to the grand opening of her new facility. She was on cloud nine because she received a Federal grant and could expand her work.

When I left her office, I was elated thinking that I had accomplishments to be proud of.

Three days later I got a phone call from her secretary. I could hardly understand her between her sobs. "Ray, Mrs. Orton was driving to her new office and an oncoming car went left of center and hit her head on. She was killed instantly."

I was dumbstruck. She continued, "I know how close you were. The wake is Friday at Davis' Funeral Home."

All I could say was, "thank you."

The old burning puzzlement of God's plan of things flamed up again, and I asked. "Why would You, who knows and controls everything, let this special person gain prestige and a position to help so many lost and needing souls, die? I am sick of the old rhetoric, have faith. That's the church's answer to all unanswerable questions."

I had to quit my line of thought. It never got me anywhere and never would, except to put negative thoughts in my brain.

Marilyn, our three children and I went to the funeral parlor. We knelt at her casket and said our prayers. We talked to the girls from her office, then sat in the back of the room.

A side door opened and I watched a woman enter the room and walk toward me, I felt my jaw drop and my heart stop—it was Mrs. Orton. I felt like I was in a twilight zone or a time warp. I looked at the casket, then at Marilyn and our children. Their eyes were like saucers. They saw her too.

She leaned forward and extended her hand. I was afraid to reach, expecting to grasp air.

I quickly looked around the room to see if others shared my hallucination.

The tall red head spoke. "You must be Ray. My sister has spoken about you both so much, I feel we are old friends."

My mouth was still open as she answered my confused look.

"I'm sorry if I startled you, we are identical twins."

I finally felt my heart start to beat again and stammered. "It is a pleasure to meet you. I think the world of your sister and when I saw her-you walk into the room, well, I never realized that identical twins were so...identical."

"Yes. We had a great time in college. No one could tell us apart."

We talked for a few minutes and after she left Marilyn said, "I felt like I was talking to a ghost. Her hair, smile, mannerisms and voice were exactly like her sister's."

I think about her often with fond memories and appreciation.

Weeks later, at work, my private line rang and I answered, "Plain Dealer, can I help you?"

"Raymond, it's Aunt Betty." I smiled. Her voice was unmistakable.

"Hi sweetheart. Is that red headed Irishman giving you any problems?"

"Are you kidding? He likes my cooking too much. Raymond, my new stove isn't right and the store keeps giving me the run around."

I called the store and asked to have the manager call me at the Plain Dealer. That name carried a lot of weight. The call was returned quickly and the problem corrected the next day. My aunt and Uncle Red were childless. I was the only family they had that cared. I handled their needs as best I could. My reward was some great Hungarian cooking that I would pick up after work. They lived close to the Plain Dealer and I would occasionally take them home for a weekend visit. Red suffered a slight stroke and was home in a week.

Several months later I made my usual Sunday morning call to them from the P.D., no answer. They sometimes overslept and went to a later mass. I called several times before I went home at noon. I called again about three, still no answer. I had a premonition and called their neighbor. He broke into their home and found them in their bedroom in a pool of urine and defecation. When we got to the hospital I learned Red suffered another stroke Friday night. When aunt Betty tried to lift him off the floor, she suffered a devastating stroke. They lay helpless Friday night, Saturday, Saturday night and Sunday until five p.m. They would never see their home again and Aunt Betty would never speak again. I was the only person she could communicate with. Her eyes and expressions were the same as words to me.

The next four years were a blur to Marilyn and me. A lot of pleading and some understanding social workers helped me arrange for them to be in the same room. They spent six months in City Hospital and another six months in Broadview Sanatorium and the next three years in a nursing home forty-five miles from my home. There were closer places, but Marilyn and I wouldn't leave our worst enemy in them. We visited them three and four times a week. The sixty-mile round trip to work and then another ninety miles round trip to visit them began to take its toll on my health.

Whenever I considered skipping a visit, I would remember Uncle Red's words, "Raymond, you don't know how much your visits mean. You give us credibility. No one has visitors like we do."

We would bring coffee and dozens of donuts. By the time we parked and got to their room, groups of patients were waiting for treats. It was my aunt and uncle, but Marilyn was there every second washing their bottoms, making sure their clothes were clean and cooking for them. All that plus getting me up every morning, three kids ready for school and all the man's work around the house, both inside and out. Fix the plumbing, shelves, broken windows and screens, bicycles, mow the lawn, weed the beds, sweep the walks and shovel the snow. How could I say I was tired? I figured with rest my endurance would return but I didn't know about 'Post Polio Syndrome.'

The partner in the nursery was unhappy because I spent so much time with them. One day he was exceptionally angry. I tried to explain, "What else can I do, Dan? She is my Dad's sister."

"Let them die!" he snarled. A few weeks later, Aunt Betty did die. Uncle Red died a few months later.

At his funeral, his niece approached me sobbing with accusations. "You kept me from seeing them?"

Shocked, I asked what she meant. Between sobs she continued. "We couldn't find them."

"But," I tried to explain, "they were in two Cleveland hospitals for a year and I never saw you once, let alone three years in Ashtabula."

She continued wailing. "We were so close until you stuck your nose in their life and hid them."

I tried to stay calm. "Hid them? All you had to do is call the hospital. They knew where they were."

She huffed and puffed and stormed away. Aunt Betty's words rang in my ear. "Ray, everyone comes around professing love, but they never asked if we needed a loaf of bread or a ride to church or ask us to eat at their house. Never give the key to my house to anyone."

The very day after they were admitted in the hospital, this same woman somehow managed to find my telephone number. She said sweetly. "If you give me the key to her house, we can take care of it until they return."

She was unhappy when I said I would take care of things. She must have thought I profited somehow. Aunt Betty willed her home to me, but it had to be sold and the government took the money so they could stay in nursing homes.

I began dozing at my desk. Neil, my assistant would nudge me. "Ray, you're falling asleep while we're talking. Something must be wrong. You should see a doctor."

A couple days later, while driving home from work I fell asleep and drifted into the left lane forcing a car unto the berm. His horn woke me.

"My God, Ray, you could have killed that family, and if they hadn't been there you would have gone across the medium into oncoming traffic." I did not tell, Marilyn of this miracle. She had enough to worry about.

When I got home I backed into the garage, opened my door, and backed to my spare wheelchair. The kitchen door opened and the daily ritual with my devoted Terrier commenced. At breakneck speed she flew out the kitchen door around my chair, leaped into my car, up on my lap and her nose went straight into my shirt pocket. I always saved her a goodie from my lunch. After she devoured it, I was rewarded with many kisses.

I slid across my board onto my chair and wheeled into the kitchen.

"Something smells awfully good."

"I decided to make cabbage rolls. You're ten minutes late and I thought Mitzi was going to scratch a hole in the window looking for you."

I was suspicious. Cabbage rolls are usually a Sunday meal. I was right as, Marilyn followed with, "we, a, have a problem. I got a call from the Principal at St. Gabe's."

"What did John do now?"

"The nun said they couldn't handle him anymore."

"What did you say?"

"Nothing, I made an appointment for *you* to talk to her tomorrow at four o'clock."

"Thanks a lot."

"You know I get pushed around."

"Did she say why?"

"No. You'll find out tomorrow."

My incident on the way home had to wait in line.

The next day at four the Nun sat in my car.

"Raymond, I'm very sorry about this. We talked about John before. He's not a bad boy but he is too hyper. He disrupts his classes and doesn't want to learn. David and Debbie are doing fine."

I listened, worrying what would happen to John in a less strict environment. She continued, "I'm afraid John will have to leave the school."

Then she said something that angered me. "We have a long waiting list of young children that want to learn and, John is denying them a chance."

"Sister, I only went to the fifth grade in Catholic school but those few years set my pattern for life. Many of Gods teachings are burned deep in my soul. One of the fundamental teachings I remember, was about, God tending His sheep. If one strayed, He would leave the flock to save the one. Is that still a teaching of our religion?"

I looked at the Nun. She looked out the window for several minutes. She finally turned and with a slight smile said. "Okay, we'll give John another chance."

That chance gave John time to mature. He is now a wonderful father, successful in his chosen field and a considerate, loving son. Again, the wisdom in the Bible proved itself.

Our children were always the tallest in their class, David, the second child was extra tall. Each child holds compartments in my heart that I wouldn't trade for anything on this earth. One incident that always brings me a smile was on a warm day in July. He was kneeling in a freshly tilled bed planting Rhododendron liners. He was twelve years old and the sweat was running down over his freckles. He looked up and saw his buddy riding back and forth at the end of our drive. I knew what he was thinking and said, "David, do you realize how lucky you are?"

He looked at me as he wiped his forehead. "Lucky," he answered. "How?"

"Look at Donald. Poor kid doesn't have a thing to do but a ride his bicycle in circles. You are luckier than you know."

He looked at his friend, then at the plants waiting to be planted, then at me.

I wanted him to keep that thought, so before he could answer I followed with, "you'll be done in fifteen minutes, and then you can go riding."

I had to wheel away so he couldn't see my smile. The picture of him kneeling with the trowel in his hand, and his big brown eyes looking at me, is in my storehouse forever.

His height and coordination in basketball won him the Most Valuable Player award from grade school through college.

His games, during my failing health, keep me going. It was something to look forward to. It was a therapy for me.

My progressing weakness gave me many warning signs.

One was the increasing instances, were nightmares. I would dream I was crawling through a deep tunnel trying to escape to the surface and air. Then I would get wedged, unable to move or breathe. I would panic, knowing death was inevitable. Other times I was put in a coffin and lowered into the ground. I heard the dirt covering the coffin and the oxygen depleting. The realization that I was trapped and dying was horrible. I would wake up in a cold sweat gasping for air. I would try to stay awake, afraid I would return to the same nightmare. The dreams and terror increased.

I still don't understand why I failed to recognize the signs.

David got a grant to a Catholic high school. The basketball games were sold out with standing room only. They won the district championship. We couldn't afford to send our daughter, so she worked at the high school cleaning toilets. Although she felt it was degrading at the time, it did build character. She now speaks of it with pride to her children.

My exhaustion increased. I kept telling myself things would get better. It is easy to sell yourself because you know the strings that influence you, and you pull them.

Then, the fateful morning. The alarm shattered the quiet with its three-thirty wake up song. Marilyn usually slept through the first ringing.

I turned it off and quickly returned my arm to the warmth of the electric blanket. "You'll never make it, Ray." I tried to convince myself. "Your body can't even think of moving, call in sick."

I pulled the warm covers over my ears. "See how good it feels. Call in, dummy. Others do."

50 YEARS OF MIRACLES

I reveled at the thought of sleeping all day, but my conscience nagged at me until I nudged Marilyn.

"It's time, Mare."

She moaned and rolled over. I waited a few minutes hoping I would fall asleep.

I nudged her again. "Mare, the alarm went off."

"I heard it. I was hoping it was a dream."

She rolled out of bed and headed for the kitchen to turn on the coffee machine. I threw the cover back and pulled my corset off my wheelchair. I rolled on my stomach, centered the corset on my spine, rolled back, hooked it and put on my trousers. Marilyn returned, grabbed my hand and helped me sit up. She put on my socks, shoes and shirt then asked, "want a push to the bathroom?" I nodded, no.

The ten-foot trip took every ounce of strength I could muster. With my elbows on the sink I squinted at myself in the mirror.

"You look like hell. How are you going to drive into Cleveland and work all day when you can't even keep your eyes open?"

My head felt like it weighed a hundred pounds, so I rested my chin on my hands. "Well, you felt the same yesterday and made it, so I guess you can today, too."

Marilyn came in with a bowl of cereal and cup of coffee. I finished my cereal with my eyes shut then downed the steaming coffee. I shaved, brushed my teeth, combed my hair then rested my head on my hands again. Then in the distance I heard a voice. It was Marilyn.

"Hey! Are you sleeping?"

"Who? Me? No!"

"Bologna, I heard you snoring, do you want me to drive you in?"

"What a girl," I thought. "All you have to do and without batting and eye you offer to drive a hundred and twenty miles today. What did I ever do to deserve you?"

I answered her. "No thanks, another cup of coffee and I'll be all

147

right. I would appreciate it if you'd start the van and put the heater on." I wish now I had let her drive me in.

"Okay," she answered and left.

I wheeled out to the family room and she was pouring me a second cup of coffee. I took a few sips. "Either the rug is getting thicker or I'm getting weaker."

Again she offered. "Sure you don't want me to drive you in?"

"No thanks, I'm awake now."

She went outside and as I finished my second cup, she returned. "The lift is down and I moved the seat back for you."

"You're a doll. Now go to sleep for a couple hours."

She kissed me and I wheeled to the van. I backed onto the lift and my right elbow held the toggle switch back while the electric motors lifted me level with the van floor. I backed next to the driver's seat, removed the left arm of my wheelchair, put my sliding board between my chair and the seat, then slid over. I grabbed the steering wheel and swivelled the seat until it locked forward. I reached under the right side of the seat and pushed the toggle switch forward. The seat started its two-foot travel down and toward the dash. I moved my feet with my hand until I was in the driving position. I hooked my seat belt, activated the switch on the dash that shut the lift doors and started my thirty-mile drive. Traffic is negligible at four thirty a.m. and my mind kept busy planning the day's activities. Everything went as usual until I exited the inner-belt onto Superior Avenue.

Then the nightmare started.

I was five short blocks from the Plain Dealer.

Suddenly, my seat started to move back. I quickly reached for the toggle switch under my seat, only to find it unresponsive.

My seat kept moving back, and to add to my horror the engine began to roar at full throttle.

"Jesus, Raymond. What's happening?"

I glanced at my speedometer as I drove through the first intersection.

TWENTY-FIVE MILES PER HOUR!

The seat finally stopped all the way up and back. I was laying on my knees barely able to reach the hand brake and steering wheel. I couldn't exert enough pressure on the hand brake, and the van kept picking up speed. I went through the next intersection and a red light, at—.

THIRTY MILES PER HOUR!

I heard panic in my voice as I cried out. "This has got to be a dream! It can't be happening!"

I tried to calm myself.

"Think, Raymond! THINK! You just went through another red light and you're lucky no one was in the intersection, and you're now going…"

THIRTY-FIVE MILES PER HOUR!

"You MUST do something, but WHAT! You can't reach the ignition or the gear shift and the damn engine is screaming. By the time you get to Ninth Street you'll be doing ninety, and you know people never look when they cross the street because they assume cars will stop."

The picture of my van grinding multitudes of bodies under its huge frame struck more terror in my heart. I thought. "This only happens in the movies."

"Wait a minute, Ray. The movies! Remember when Cary Grant was going down a hill out of control, you always said he should hit something before he was going too fast. Well, THAT is your only option. YOU HAVE TO SMASH INTO SOMETHING! And QUICK! There is a light pole on the corner of Eighteenth Street. That has to be your target."

I looked at my speedometer as I approached the intersection.

FORTY MILES PER HOUR!

"Please, God, let the light be green and no one crossing."

I got to the intersection and spotted my target.

"Oh, no!" I moaned. "It has a huge concrete base. It won't give and inch."

I chickened out and roared through the intersection.

"Ray!" I yelled at myself. "You have to stop this death wagon, NOW!"

I felt guilty for putting my fears ahead of innocent lives.

"Look. There is a station wagon parked by the curb by itself, and It looks empty. You have room to pull behind it and hit it square, at least you won't roll over."

I resigned myself to the deed.

"You're *it*, wagon," I said with the determination of a Kamikaze pilot.

I swung in and lined myself the best I could with my speeding van. I watched the station wagon as I quickly closed upon it. My heart pounded violently as I steeled myself for the impact. I shut my eyes at the last second.

I heard the sickening sound of steel smashing against steel. Then, silence. Dead silence.

"Am I dead?" I asked myself.

"Open your eyes and see where you are."

I was afraid to find out.

"You have to know which world you're in. Open them."

I slowly forced them open. I was in the van and the engine was running at a smooth idle.

"What the hell?" I started to say. "The engine was just screaming. You must be dreaming, shake your head and you'll wake up."

I shook it, but nothing changed. I slowly lifted my head to look at the wagon I hit.

"WHAT!" I exclaimed in total confusion. Nothing was in front of me. I looked to my left and traffic was going by like nothing happened. I looked to my right and saw that I was in front of a fire station.

"Why weren't people responding to the noise?" I asked myself.

A pain in my back reminded me of my folded position. I tried to straighten myself up, but my arms weren't strong enough to lift the weight of my upper body.

I looked forward again and discovered the missing wagon. I hit it so hard it skidded fifty feet into the next parked car. Its back was smashed and boxes it was carrying were hanging out the smashed rear window.

A frightening thought then painted a horrible picture in my mind.

"If that wagon is smashed that bad, what about your front end? Are you leaking gas? Will you catch fire?"

Even in my grave situation, I had to smile.

"Wouldn't that be a headline for tomorrow morning's Plain Dealer. Man dies in fire in front of Fire Department."

My smile disappeared quickly and I walked my fingers along the hand brake to the steering wheel and along the spoke above the keys. I had to drop my hand and hope I could catch the keys. I would only get one try. I said a silent prayer and dropped my hand. My finger caught in the ring and I shut off the engine.

The success of that action didn't last long as I became aware that I was struggling to breathe. My position was restricting the ability of my weak muscles to give me enough oxygen.

I knew if I panicked my breathing would become worse, and I would pass out—and die.

"Ray, attract attention. Blow the horn."

I blasted the horn repeatedly. After five minutes the battery went dead.

My mind was overwhelmed as I ran out of options. I prayed and felt a calmness as I resigned myself to the inevitable.

"And God," I whispered. "Please watch over Marilyn and the children."

Then I heard a tapping at my window. It was a fireman. He was leaving work and noticed my smashed van. I motioned to him and he opened the door.

"Please sit me up," I whispered.

"I'm not sure if I should move you, I'll call the paramedics."

"I have to sit up so I can breathe," I pleaded. "I won't make it till they get here."

Reluctantly, he slowly pushed me up to a sitting position.

Without the pressure on my chest, I started to suck in wonderful life-sustaining air.

Within minutes the paramedics were there and strapped me to a board keeping me in a sitting position. They gently lifted me out of the driver's door and onto a Gurney.

They loaded me into their vehicle and delivered me to a local hospital. By the time the x-rays were developed, Marilyn was there. The x-rays were okay and I was released. Marilyn had a local ambulance service take me home. With tears in her eyes she held my hand and said,

"I should have insisted to drive you today."

My exhaustion continued. A hospital bed was set up in our family room so Marilyn could continue her chores while watching me. I was still aching from the accident and stayed in bed most of the day. I continuously drifted off to sleep even while being fed. Nights were blurs of half sleep and bad dreams. Marilyn was exhausted from the regular care of house, yard, children and constant care and worrying about me. If she sat down after finishing supper dishes, she would be out like a light. A tree could fall on the house and she would never hear it, but the slightest moan from me and she was up in a flash.

This particular night after everyone went to bed, I started my nightly routine of on/off sleep. The nightmares, for some reason, were more severe and unusually painful. When I opened my eyes, I saw Marilyn's solemn look. I was puzzled by the strange surroundings. I turned my head to the left and saw a tall unfamiliar priest.

My wife answered my look. "This is Father Tom Johns, from Saint Gabriel's."

"Hi, Ray. This is my first night at St. Gabe's and I received a call to rush to Lake County Hospital at three a.m. and didn't know where it was." He smiled and continued, "you gave me an exciting first day on the job, but I'm glad to see you're back with us. We'll talk later." He rested his hand on my forehead, said a prayer and left.

I tried to shake the fog from my head. I spotted a clock on the wall. It read four thirty. I tried to swallow and my throat exploded with pain. I opened my mouth to cry out but found I couldn't speak. I looked back at Marilyn. She saw the pain and question in my eyes and stood aside.

Dr. Rutherford stepped forward and spoke. "Hi, Ray, you gave us quite a scare, but you'll be all right now."

I felt my forehead wrinkle from further puzzlement as he continued. "About three a.m. your wife found you in a pool of sweat and couldn't wake you. She called the rescue squad and they rushed you to the hospital. We had a tough time getting the tube down your nose and throat. You fought against it to a point where we almost did a tracheotomy. You were turning blue, but we finally got it down. You won't be able to talk and the tube will feel uncomfortable. An infection in your lungs is keeping them from absorbing oxygen."

He pointed to an I.V. dripping a solution into a tube that ran to my arm, and he continued.

"We're mixing an antibiotic with your I.V., and oxygen with your ventilator. Now that you're awake, we'll roll you on your sides and give you percussion treatments. The respiratory therapists will cup their hands and hit you on the back to loosen the secretions in your lungs."

After two weeks of medicine and therapy my lungs cleared up, the tubes were removed and I returned home.

I regained some strength but couldn't handle the long drive to visit my aunt and uncle. I felt terrible about it. My children made trips in our place with the coffee and donuts.

By fall, Marilyn saw I wasn't improving and took me to the Cleveland Clinic. They checked my blood gasses and found them dangerously low, and I was admitted. They had no choice but to put a trac into my throat, and hook me up to a ventilator. I was devastated, but again, no alternatives.

When they wheeled me to the operating room to insert a trac, I was semi-conscience, but could hear the doctors talk as they numbed my throat.

"Do you feel this?" The first doctor asked.

I nodded no.

The second doctor followed with, "you'll feel a little pressure, Ray." Then he said to a nurse. "Keep the oxygen mask over his nose."

The first doctor spoke. "There, the cut is done, hand me the trac, nurse." She did.

There was a moment's pause, then he followed with. "Hey! It doesn't want to go in."

The second doctor said. "Let me try." After a couple grunts he agreed. "No, it doesn't! What size did you order?"

"Number eight Shiley."

"Number eight! No wonder it doesn't fit."

"It should, this guy's six-six."

"Yeah, but he doesn't weigh three hundred pounds."

"Okay, so what do we do? He's open and bleeding."

I looked at the nurse holding the oxygen mask. Her eyes spoke what she dare not say. She squeezed my hand forcing a smile.

The doctors were excited and didn't realize I was listening to the circus. The routine sounded funny, until I asked myself,

"What are you laughing at? They're talking about your throat and your blood."

I began to panic!

"Stay calm, Ray." I told myself. "Think about the nurse's deep blue eyes."

I just started to calm down when the first doctor ordered a nurse. "Run down to the stock room and get a number six Shiley with a cuff, STAT!"

I hated the word STAT. It always meant EMERGENCY! The nurse left the room quickly.

The second young doctor put a hand on my shoulder and tried to comfort me.

"It won't be long. Hang in there."

"Keep calm, Raymond," I kept repeating to myself.

I was doing okay until the first doctor asked his partner. "What if they don't have a number six?"

A dead silence engulfed the room.

"Oh Sweet Jesus," I moaned to myself. "You've got two of the Three Stooges here." I had to chuckle to myself. "At least there aren't three of them."

Just then the nurse ran into the room and handed the doctor a box. It took her a couple breaths before she could speak. "A number—six Shiley—with a cuff."

A few weeks after the fiasco, with air and oxygen feeding my starved lungs, I began regaining my strength. I was in intensive care for almost two months. The hospital was thirty miles from home and Marilyn drove the sixty miles every day. She would get up at six a.m., pack lunches, get three children off to school, clean, wash and be at the hospital before noon with a home cooked meal. After my morning routines, the nurses would get me up in my wheelchair by eleven. I would sit by my window that overlooked the hospital entrance and watch for Marilyn. My world was in limbo until I saw my angel walking out of the parking garage. I would think, "Marilyn, how I wish I could find the words that would express the true depth of my feelings for you, but mere words can't come near what I feel. Without you, my life would be—an empty shell."

When she entered my room and we embraced I would say. "You are my sunshine and I love you." She would smile and I would think, "I wish I could be a Rembrandt of words so I could speak you a masterpiece expressing how you make me feel."

The nurses were very good to us. Every day we would travel the hospital corridors trying to wean me from my breathing machine. A nurse would push my chair and Marilyn would use the Ambu bag to occasionally squeeze a few breaths of air through my trac. The antibiotics and weeks of struggle began paying off. I amazed the nurses, respiratory therapists, doctors and myself. After six weeks I was able to breathe on my own with a cap over my trac tube.

Finally after two more weeks the doctor said I could go home, with a ventilator.

I asked the doctor if I could use a rocking bed instead of a ventilator.

He smiled. "No, Ray, your blood gasses are good and we want to keep them that way."

"But doctor, what if the rocking bed keeps my gasses steady?"

"Raymond," he insisted. "I know a ventilator is confining, but your health and strength is my prime concern."

He was a good doctor, but didn't care to discuss my views. I asked everyone at the hospital what they thought. They admitted I was doing much better than they expected, but were afraid to voice an opinion on what I should do. No one argues with doctors, except for big mouth, me. Every day for a week I tried to convince him a rocking bed would work. Every day he steamed more and more and I couldn't bring any of the staff into it for fear of their positions.

Finally, out of frustration, he asked. "What do you propose? What value do you place on your health?"

The door, I felt was open a crack. "Why not try a rocking bed for a night and check my gasses to see if they maintain their level?"

The room was quiet as he leafed through his notes. He turned to the respiratory therapist. "Do we have a rocking bed in the hospital?"

The therapist had checked a week earlier for me, but was afraid to admit it, so he answered, "ah—yes sir. That is, I think so. I've never seen one, but I've heard talk of one."

"Check it out. If we do, have maintenance clean it up and bring it here."

That afternoon they wheeled in a monstrous contraption. The floor creaked and the engineer said. "Mother of God! This thing must be made from battleship steel."

"Do you think the antique will still work?" I mused.

He raised his eyebrows. "Still work?" He pointed to the massive gears. "They mesh perfectly and hardly whisper while running. It wouldn't wear out in ten lifetimes."

"Great," I said. "I can't wait to try it."

"One problem," he injected. "It has to be geared down. At this speed it'll throw you off like a bucking bronco." He started it up and I counted thirty-five rocks per minute. Fear set in as I asked. "Think you can gear it down to nineteen per minute?"

He worked on the adjustment, then started it. I counted twenty-eight.

My heart sank further as he said, "that's the most I can adjust it. It must have another set of gears, but I couldn't find any, and I doubt if they make 'em like this any more."

There must be a way, I thought, but didn't know if the engineer took to outside suggestions. He broke the ice and asked me. "Any suggestions? You've seen more of these than I have."

I smiled. "I've ridden a few. Rodeo riders have nothing on me." I studied the gearing. It was looking hopeless until I looked at the pulley wheel on the old electric motor. "Do you think another pulley would help?"

"Not sure we have one to fit the shaft of that old motor, but I will go down and look."

I looked at Marilyn. "It's four o'clock, time's running out."

The nurses kept checking and offering words of encouragement. They brought in the supper tray and my chin dropped as I realized it was five o'clock. The engineers went home at five and it was Friday, which meant no one on duty until Monday.

"Want me to feed you?" Marilyn asked consolingly.

"No thanks, I'm not hungry."

"Hey! That looks good enough to eat." The engineer said as he walked into my room carrying a large pulley.

"I couldn't find a regular pulley to fit. Then I checked some old blowers with adjustable pulleys, and darned if I didn't find one. What took so long was I had to heat it to get it off, and I had to be careful not to ruin it."

I nearly cried with joy as I watched him put it on and adjusted it a couple times.

"There you are son," he said proudly. "Nineteen per-minute."

I shook his hand and tried to give him some money. He smiled and shook his head. "No thanks. Glad I could do it. The nurses told me how important it was to you." As he left, he finished with, "Sure hope it does what you want."

It was the best supper I ever ate.

At nine o'clock Marilyn and the nurses put me in bed.

The nurse said, "Ray, the doctor left orders to check your blood gasses every hour all night."

For a guy six foot six I have small, hard to find veins plus thirty years of needles put scars on them making them more difficult to penetrate, but nothing could dampen my spirit. She continued. "I'll put in a shunt so we won't have to stick you every hour."

"If it wasn't improper, I'd give you a kiss," I said smiling.

"So who cares." She bent over and kissed me on the cheek and she left to get the shunt.

Marilyn smiled. "Hmmm, does this go on all the time? Can I trust you with all these pretty nurses?"

To myself I said. "Here you lay, a long skinny pile of dead muscles, and she's still a bit jealous, but it does feel good."

The nurse inserted the shunt and Marilyn tucked me in. She kissed me goodnight and said she would pray that bed would do the job. She clicked my half ton giant to life and I began the nineteen rocks per minute. Marilyn stopped at the door, blew me a kiss and said, "no kissy kissy when I'm not here."

The motion of the bed made me feel like I was being rocked in my mother's arms. I fell asleep in the middle of my prayers. The nurses that took my blood each hour were so gentle and quiet I slept until the three o'clock drawing.

"I'm sorry," she said. "I didn't mean to wake you."

"You didn't wake me. I have to use the urinal. Please turn the bed off."

She did and left for a few minutes. When she returned, she said. "Your nurses that are off duty have been calling all night to check on the results."

"And?" I questioned with apprehension.

She smiled. "So far so good. We're all pulling for you. It took a lot of guts to stand up to your doctor and we still can't believe you got the bed."

The sound of the smooth running gears and the motion of the bed soon had me back in dream land. The next morning the doctor entered my room with two nurses and a respiratory therapist. He was expressionless as he leafed through my file. I studied all the faces and began to worry. Without cracking a smile he said to the therapist. "Make arrangements to get a rocking bed to his home." He turned to me. "Your blood gasses remained constant all night. When you get a rocking bed at home, we'll release you." Then, with a hint of a smile he finished with, "I'm glad it worked out for you, Ray. My main concern is to keep you out of trouble. You were lucky that we could clear up your infection. I'll remove your trac today and put in a 'button'."

"A 'button'?"

"Yes, a short tube that will keep your opening from closing. Then if you need suctioning, we won't have to operate on you again."

After he left the therapist and nurses clapped quietly and congratulated me. "You won!" They said together. Within an hour the doctor returned and replaced my long trac with a 'button'.

"Doctor," I asked. What will keep it from going down my wind pipe? It doesn't have a wide bracket like my other trac."

"Don't worry. We've never lost one yet." He gave one of his rare smiles.

Three days later, Marilyn told me the bed came in but they couldn't get it through my bedroom door. I told her to call Paul. I was fortunate to have great, talented friends. He removed the door frames and assembled the bed. My departure day arrived.

It was a warm sunny day. It seemed like half the hospital came down to see me off. Marilyn drove to the entrance, opened the automatic van doors and my beloved friend walked out on the lift and looked at all the people standing at the entrance. Mitzi's ears stood up as she listened to the city noises. Her jaws opened as she tried to bark, but nothing came out. She had been howling for me all the time I was in the hospital, and lost her voice. When I called her name, she spotted me, leaped off the lift and with her ears back ran to me. She jumped in my lap giving me a thousand kisses. My day was complete.

Two weeks later I was back in my doctor's office for a routine visit. One of my nurses and the respiratory therapist were there.

"Doctor," I started. "I am always coughing and spitting up phlegm, and my throat is always sore. This darn button keeps going deeper into my neck. Do I really need it?"

The question brought him up out of his chair.

"Do you need it? Yes, you do!"

The nurse and therapist looked like they wished they were somewhere else. He continued. "You talked me out of the ventilator, but I won't bend on removing the button. I am responsible for your health. With all the phlegm you're producing, you need an access to your lungs. It's just a matter of time, Ray." With his orders hanging in the air, he left the office.

The nurse waited until he was out of earshot. "You sure get him going. He is a brilliant doctor and sure of his convictions. I'm afraid you'll never change his mind on this one."

A month later I went in for a check up. When I got there, I was told my doctor was called out of town. I could see another doctor or make another appointment. Since it was a sixty-mile round trip, I chose to see the substitute doctor. The doctor checked me over and asked how long I have been off a ventilator.

"A couple months."

"And you still have a button?"

I realized my window was open. Dare I take it? Do I really need the button? If I run into trouble, will I be sorry I didn't listen? What will my regular doctor say when he discovers my button missing? I took a deep breath and answered casually "Yes, but I don't know why."

"Do you want it removed?"

"Sure, we can always punch another hole if needed."

"Okay, we'll take it out."

He took it out and told his nurse to put a butterfly over the opening.

"It will close up in a week. If you have any seepage, call us, otherwise, wait for your next checkup."

"Thanks doc," I said and we left.

Outside Marilyn looked at me. "Are you sure you did the right thing?"

"I don't know, but it feels better already." Within a week the opening closed. The constant soreness and phlegm became nonexistent and life was good again for over a decade.

I hit the golden age of fifty and wanted to do some traveling, but I had two big obstacles. The rocking bed had to go where I go, which was no small task. I could rent one at our planned destination, but how do I survive getting there? The motels don't supply rocking beds. I had to dust off my thinking cap. I came across a contraption called an ex-suffulation belt, which was a football sized rubber bladder. It was attached via a small hose to a mechanical air pump. When I went to bed I wore my corset. I put the bladder under my corset and lay on my side. When the pump cycled and expanded the bladder, it forced air out of my lungs. When it released the pressure, my stomach would expand sucking air into my lungs. After a week we had it working perfect. I rented a rocking bed in Florida. That obstacle was the simple one. But Marilyn did not want to leave home. She felt guilty leaving the children, even though they were married and parents themselves. The more grandchildren we had the worse she felt. I had to be the bad guy and insist we go. She shed a tub of tears the week before we left. Then after the first twenty minutes on the road, she was out like a light. When she would wake up a few hours later, her apprehension was gone. On every trip, the same scenario.

My second son, John, was going to college in Southern California taking court reporting. He met a girl and they planned marriage. Marilyn and I wanted to go to California to meet her and her family. We sat down to figure how we could do it, so I made a list. We needed a place to stay for three months that would accept two pets. We needed a rocking bed. I wasn't up to driving that far so we had to fly and we needed a van with a lift when we got there. None were available to rent. Marilyn looked at the list. "Can't anything we do, be simple? When other people want to go away, they pack a bag and go, and getting to and from their destination costs them a few hundred dollars. It cost us a few thousand, that isn't fair."

"Marilyn, when we're born, nobody promised us life would be fair." I knew my health wouldn't last forever.

"Mare, we can afford to go now so we have to do what we have to, we don't have a choice."

John got us a new condo to rent through a friend. He flew home and drove our van out. The flight out was terrible. Seats are not designed for six foot six people. Thank God the flight was only four hours. My last flight from California was eight hours. I'd never have made it this time, but we got there and had a great time. We met the girl and her family and liked them immediately.

We drove to Santa Monica. I wanted to visit my old "home" and see if any of the staff might still be there. It was twenty five years since I left C.R.C. We parked at the Pier. It was changed completely. We headed south on the boardwalk.

It was three blocks to Ocean Avenue. I looked for Muscle Beach, gone. I looked for The Cork where we used to party, gone. The boardwalk that was straight from the pier to Venus, gone. A twisting walkway lined with little shops replaced everything. We got to Ocean Avenue and my heart was broken. The California Rehabilitation Center, was also gone. All that was left was a vacant lot. A postage stamp-sized piece of dirt. I checked the street signs several times. I couldn't believe eight stories, an Olympic pool, offices, cafeteria, therapy department, pulley department and a huge lobby sat on that tiny piece of sand. The Spanish wall and entrance archway to our patio, also, gone. I was sorry I visited 1815 Ocean Front. I so wanted to keep the old picture in my memories. It felt like that eighteen months of my life never existed. It was a sad drive back to Upland and our condo.

The rest of our stay was joyful. We saw our son almost every day for the three months. I had missed him desperately. His happiness was the most important thing in my life. Marilyn and I were sad to leave him so far from home.

We are blessed that two of our children live close to us. My daughter and her family live a hundred feet away. Our grandchildren are all tall and healthy. The boys are handsome and the girl's beautiful. Our 6'8" son, David and 6'3" son, John are both healthy and our beautiful 5'11" daughter, Debbie is married to a great guy. We have lived together with each of their families for six or more months and had a wonderful relationship. When I count my blessings, I need an adding machine.

As 1980 approached, my health and stamina began decreasing. I developed a pain in my chest. Examination showed I had developed a hole in my lung. The doctor inserted a syringe into my chest cavity and removed fluid that leaked through the hole.

I babied myself and it healed, but I could tell by the doctor's concern that all was not well. Time proved I was right.

CHAPTER EIGHT

LIFE, OR

I rang my small copper bell, and Marilyn came to my bedroom.

"Ready to get up Ray? Supper is almost ready."

"Yeah, I'm tired of laying."

"I checked on you a couple times, but were sleeping."

"I didn't think I slept at all."

I pressed the control and raised the head of my electric bed.

"I'm glad I bought this Craft-A-Matic bed, my feet don't hang like on a regular hospital bed."

She shut off the ventilator on my headboard, disconnected the long tube from my trach., pushed the Hoyer lift under the bed and hooked the chains to the sling under my body. She pumped the hydraulic cylinder a dozen times until I cleared the bed. She ran my electric chair under me and lowered me onto the cushion. With a push of a button the ventilator under my chair came to life. She attached its long tube to my trach, and I could talk again.

"Remember the first time I sat in a chair after my operations?"

"God, do I. It took three nurses and me. You were blue by the time we got you in the chair and re-hooked your vent."

"I remember I couldn't draw a breath. I saw the end of my road."

"Yes, but you fooled 'em again. It took six months but now you can breathe a half hour on your own."

"You're the miracle, Marilyn. Now, you get this goofy body up, dressed and ready to go in ten minutes. My name should be Ken."

"Ha! My very own Barbie Doll," she laughed.

"And I'm here for you to play with anytime."

"Go throw some cold water on your face, and I'll finish supper."

I drove my chair into the bathroom, combed my hair, then asked my reflection. "How can she get your carcass in and out of bed four times a day all these years and still love you? Because you're handsome and charming? N-a-a. It's your smile. You devil you."

Marilyn yelled from the hallway. "Talking to yourself again?"

"Why not? At least I have someone that'll listen. Mirror, I better be careful or they'll be throwing a net over me." I moved my control and drove to the family room. Donahue was on T.V., and his program was about rape and its effect on victims. My first thoughts were anger toward the law's leniency on the perpetrators.

"They should be castrated," Marilyn said.

"So should the judges and lawyers that let 'em out. On the other hand—."

"Okay, Mr. contrary thinker, what are your thoughts?"

"I bet if doctors had a procedure to zap and destroy that part of the brain that drives these men to their perverted acts, they would line up in a heartbeat. Except for that quirk, I bet they're mostly good guys. But they know if they seek help their life is over."

"What about the ones that aren't mostly good guys?"

"Shoot 'em."

"Interesting concept."

"Marilyn, you're getting those political 'sound bites' down pat."

My attention returned to the program. Victim after victim told of their lives after the rapes. Their fears, paranoia, nightmares and changes in their systems. Psychologists discussed all aspects. All at once I felt like I was struck by a bolt of lightning.

"OH MY GOD!" I exclaimed.

"What?" Marilyn asked.

"OH MY GOD!" I repeated.

"Ray! What's the matter?"

"They're talking about me."

"You?"

"Yes, now I understand. After all these years, I *finally* understand."

"Understand what?"

"Understand why I hate being around drunks. Understand why drinking makes me nauseous. Understand why I prefer women doctors, and why I cringe when a man puts his hand on my shoulder. And my dreams, I'm always dreaming men are trying to catch and seduce me. Good friends, and even relatives. I never could understand why I dreamed such crazy things."

Marilyn sat next to me. "You never told me."

"I guess I was ashamed. I can't believe all these years and I never figured it out—till right now."

"You've overcome so many things. Your strength has been your ability to bury negative thoughts."

"And all this time they were fermenting and pouring their poisons into my body and mind."

From that day on, things changed. Understanding *why* one feels a certain emotion is a genuine healer. My respect for psychologists and psychiatrists soared.

167

Several weeks later about ten p.m., I was at my desk. Marilyn as usual, fell asleep watching t.v. about nine. The dog barked at a raccoon and woke her. As she headed for bed, she found me at my desk.

"Ray, what are you typing that's so important? You've been at your desk all day and should be resting before your operation."

I couldn't tell my wife what was so important. She has suffered through so much with me already. "Don't worry Marilyn, I'm taking my afternoon naps and you're feeding me like a horse."

"And you're still skin and bones."

"You go back to bed. I'll be there soon."

As she left, she pleaded. "Please, not too late tonight."

I thought of the conversation with my doctor a week earlier. His eyes gave depth to his words. "Ray, I've always been straight with you. A double Pneumothorax is a lot for a healthy person. Being a polio quad with weak breathing muscles, well, we're just not sure what your system can take."

I hated to ask, but I did. "What does the operation involve?"

"An incision is made under each arm between two ribs. The ribs are pried apart and the surgeon reaches into the lungs. If the holes are not repairable, we will scrape the cavity walls raw and the pieces of lung will grow to the walls. You won't have a lung cavity anymore."

I was really sorry I asked, but I felt I had to lighten the situation. "Great, that means no more pleurisy pains. The lungs won't scrape on the walls anymore, right?"

He smiled. "You always find something good in any situation. You remind me of the optimistic boy that got a ton of horse manure for Christmas. When asked what he got for Christmas, he smiled and answered, I got a pony but haven't found him yet."

I completed the letter I was writing, then read it:

Dearest Mother;

I have had this letter in my mind for a long time. Now I must put it on paper. I am so sorry for the misery and pain I have caused you. Only after I had children of my own could I comprehend the magnitude and depth of heart ache, I have caused you. I truly wish I had died that first night in City Hospital.

You somehow survived Dad's early death and you would have survived my death. Then you could have enjoyed your grandchildren. Joe and Muncie would have been there for you.

You had a lifetime of suffering, struggle and sacrifice. You were so poor, Joe had to live with relatives for several years. When Joe was ten, a wealthy family arranged to adopt him. But the day they came to pick him up you ran into the field sobbing. Dad decided not to go through with the adoption, and then, my unscheduled arrival, ironically on Easter Sunday. To make things worse, my brother and sister were good quiet children. I was the little shit, always causing everyone problems I never meant to.

You were so strong. To save a few dollars for your family you refused Novocain when you had your teeth pulled. Oh God, Mother, all you did for us. None of us deserved you. I so wish I could have been the son to you that I should have been. By the time I was getting old enough to know better, Dad died in that accident. I'm glad for the two years we lived together. You were so lonely I wouldn't stay out after midnight because I knew you worried. I thank God for that little time I could give you.

Then, on my nineteenth birthday I tore out your heart. I have a picture of us the first time the nurses rolled me on my stomach. I felt like a Sherman tank was on my back pushing me into the mattress. You were sitting next to the bed with your hands on my bony back. Looking at your, son—excuse me, I have to wipe my tears.—. They aren't tears for me. They are for you and how you must have ached having to look at your six-foot six inch skeleton son now weighing ninety-eight pounds. Lord, Lord, Lord.

I remember the day my ten-year-old son David was climbing a tree. When I wheeled outside, I saw him and yelled for him to come down, carefully. A branch broke and he fell thirty feet breaking branches all the way down. With a sickening thud, his body disappeared into the deep weeds around the tree. There was no movement and I couldn't get to him with my wheelchair. I couldn't breathe or feel until I finally saw him stand. I would have to multiply that feeling by at least a million, to understand how you felt looking at your son.

First Dad, then Muncie, then me. I was the final straw that finally broke your wonderful strong heart.

Six years later you were diagnosed with bone cancer and given six months to live. Your reward for being such a good mother was to lose your leg at the hip. You fought so valiantly. If I hadn't destroyed so much of your heart I'm sure you would have beat it, or never got it in the first place. For three years you suffered. I can still hear the cries of pain you tried to muffle every day and every night. The shots that Marilyn gave you lasted four hours at first. The last year every fifteen minutes didn't help. How you prayed for death.

I prayed and prayed until bitterness and hatred of God consumed me. I heard myself crying and screaming. "God damn you, Christ! Why can't you let her die in peace? Dying I can understand, but do you have to torture her to death. Where is your fucking mercy? If any human did this to my mother, I would cut them to pieces slowly, with no regrets. You are in charge of the Universe. You can do anything. Why did You let this continue? If You are there and didn't help her, then, You are no God I want to know. I've read and been preached to about Your miracles, Bullshit! This woman deserved a miracle, or at least peace in death. My religion teaches us about Christ suffering on the cross. My mother suffered at least a hundred times more and longer than, You did."

As I read my profanity to God my soul swirled in confusion and shame, but I continued reading.

I may be with you soon. To see you and Dad would bring me great joy. For Marilyn's sake, I hope it won't be until I can prepare her and the children's future.

Your heart is so great, I know you forgive me for the pain I have caused you.

I just hope I can forgive myself. Keep an eye out for me.

Your loving son, Raymond.

As we drove out our driveway the next morning I looked at the geese on our pond and wondered if I'd ever see my home and yard again. The leaves on the wet pavement brought back the painful memory of October 11, 1948.

"You're awfully quiet Ray."

"Thinking about when Dad was killed. I drove the Caddy to school that day. He was in the pick up truck when he was hit. If he had been in the heavy car—."

"You can't blame—"

"I know. That's what everyone told me, but I can't stop wondering." For weeks after he died, I'd stop at the cemetery almost every day and sit on the ground above him. I'd pray and talk to him. "Dad, give me a sign and I'll dig you up with my bare hands." I knew it wasn't logical, but I felt nothing was beyond God's will. It's funny, the first week wasn't bad but as time went on, it got worse, much worse. At breakfast I'd look at his big coffee cup expecting him to walk into the kitchen any minute. When I was plowing, I'd look around, expecting to see him driving his green pickup to check on my progress. His corncob pipes, the big maple he loved to sit under. Every corner of the nursery held his image. God, how I missed him, and still do.

"We're here," Marilyn said as we pulled into the hospital parking lot. We checked in at the desk and Marilyn wheeled me to Intensive Care.

My doctor greeted us. "We arranged to give you the end unit. It has a cot for Marilyn and you're out of the main stream of activity."

"Thanks for fixing it so I can stay with him," Marilyn said.

"You've taken care of him for thirty years. The nurses will be grateful for the help."

"I sure am a pain in the gluteus." I added jokingly.

As my young doctor left Marilyn shook her head "It'll take a while for him to get used to you."

"Gee Marilyn, am I that different?"

"Yes."

I brought my own Rocking Bed to the hospital. They've become rare since the Salk Vaccine. Every worker in the hospital stopped to see my relic.

I had called, unsuccessfully, all over the country trying to find a post-Polio that had a Pneumothorax. [Holes in the lungs]. We were flying blind. I had to choose between two doctors, so I questioned the nurses. They know the doctors, and if they can trust you not to quote them, they will give their opinions.

They all agreed that one doctor had great bedside manners. The second was older, but gruff. The nurses confided he was hell to work with. My question to each was who would they want to operate on them. They all agreed, "the tough geezer." Since I wasn't looking for a lifetime companion, I chose him.

On his first procedure I found out they were right.

He inserted a three-quarter inch tube between my ribs into each lung cavity. A root canal without Novocain wouldn't have hurt as much. A week later I got his prognosis.

"Raymond, your lungs aren't healing. Surgery is scheduled for tomorrow morning, so we'll remove the tubes now."

"Doctor," I blurted out as the memory of the insertions sent lightning through my brain. "Think I can have a stronger shot for this? They were a bit rough going in."

A nurse offered, "I'll run to get one."

He replied sternly. "No need, they'll pull right out."

The pity I saw in the nurse's eyes told me to hold on to something as she slipped her hand into mine. It was without a doubt, one of the worst pains I ever experienced. I expected to see my lung hanging on the end of the tube. Before I could gather my senses, he said. "See, came right out. Now for the other one."

Thirty-nine swear words started to pour out of my mouth, but the second paralyzing shock shut down all my body functions and by the time I could speak, he was gone.

"God All mighty!" I said dazed. "Come out easy! He pulled so hard my body lifted off the bed!".

The head nurse suggested, "your chart says you can have medication upon request."

I requested.

Marilyn asked if she could be present during surgery to help keep all my body parts on the operating table. She explained that both knees were fractured and they wouldn't straighten out, but we were told hospital policy wouldn't allow it.

My optimism and belief in God were severely challenged after the first operation. When I regained consciousness, I was on my rocking bed. The motion that once lulled me like a baby in his mother's arms, was now far from adequate.

When the foot of the bed was down, gravity pulled the patient's stomach down letting air in the lungs. When the head of the bed was down gravity pushed the stomach against the lungs forcing air out.

The doctors saw me struggling and gasping for air. I wanted to tell them to increase the pitch, and speed up the number of "rocks" per minute, but I was unable to communicate, and passed out. When I woke up, I had a tube down my throat, pumping air into my lungs. The next week was a blur.

My good news continued. The other lung needed the same operation. "Do it now," I communicated. I figured I couldn't be any worse. Boy, was I wrong.

When I woke up after the second operation, the first thing I saw was all of my family. I thought I was in a casket in a funeral home being viewed by mourners. My eyes turned to the left and there was a bank of machines with dozens of flashing lights and dials that weren't there before.

My brother-in-law, a doctor, was the first to speak.

"Ray, they ran into some problems, but you're okay now. They have monitors on you so they can make sure everything stays as it should."

In movies when those words were spoken you immediately knew someone was in deep shit, but Pete's voice was so calm and assuring, I smiled.

"That's the smile we're looking for. You'll be okay kid."

Despite the gravity of the situation my wonderful brain told me, "this too will be pass."

But I soon found I couldn't draw an ounce of air on my own and that I would die fast if I wasn't connected to a ventilator. The realization that my life, as I knew it, was over. Depression overwhelmed me. Not for myself, but for my wife. I always knew my condition was a lot for my wife. In the past, after she got me up and finished my bathroom stuff, I got out of her hair until two p.m. I'd lay down until she got me up at five, then to bed at eleven p.m. Once in bed I would sleep until she got me up at seven a.m.

Now, the limited hours she had without worrying was gone. In the past I could always find something positive to think about. The smallest straw I would grip tenaciously, but now I couldn't find a trace of hope. It took every ounce of mental strength I could muster to smile and hide the anxiety my heart was suffering.

I had tubes running to a dozen places in my body. When the nurses wanted to roll me on my sides, I begged to postpone the ordeal. My pleas fell on deaf ears as four people would arrange my tubes and roll me onto rows of staples. I cried to myself and pleaded to God. "Why didn't you let me die? The pain never stops. The words from

Old Man River, "I'm tired of living but afraid of dying." Covered my feelings.

Weeks of long days and longer nights passed with agonizing slowness. I tried to let Marilyn sleep, but when I would ring for the nurses she would hear the click and wake up. The operations, the dozens of staples, the tubes in my groin, neck, arms and throat plus my arthritic knees in one position all sang a scenario of pain and discomfort that kept me from sleeping.

I asked to see my brother-in-law. That evening he sat next to my bed.

"Pete, I have a very special favor to ask. I hate to put you on the spot, but I don't have anyone else to turn to. I believe my future, for all practical purposes, is over."

I didn't always see eye to eye with my brother-in-law, but as always happens with age and maturity, my opinion changed. I began to understand the life he led as a doctor was more consuming and demanding then I could first comprehend. I studied his face as I talked. There was true compassion in his eyes. I wondered how many times he was called upon in crucial life and death situations. And, each time, how much of himself died along with his beloved patients.

He listened silently as I continued. "I don't care for myself, but I worry for Marilyn. I'm beyond repair now, but I also know it can get worse. I signed a 'Right to Die' form and I want to make sure it's carried out if I become unable to speak for myself. I talked to Marilyn and my children. They cried but finally agreed. I fear they may falter when the time comes and the plug *must* be pulled."

He nodded, "I understand."

I continued. "One more favor. I would like to dictate a note to my family. If I die, please give it to them."

"I don't believe it will be needed, but I will be glad to do what you wish."

Pete had a gift of saying just enough. He didn't preach or argue trying to change my mind. He respected my requests and my respect for him continued to grow.

My heart bled for Marilyn. She knew I needed constant care and the nurses couldn't sit by my side every minute. My legs had to be moved many times each and every hour. Thank God for my daughter Debbie. She came into the hospital every day and relieved Marilyn so she could go home to shower, clean, pay bills and take care of the dogs. Debbie would stay overnight occasionally so Marilyn could get a night's sleep. She had three young children, a husband and her own house to take care of. Her husband took over the household duties so she could be with me. As she fed me supper one evening, I started to laugh.

"What's so funny, Dad?"

"I just thought of the time when you were in the eighth grade and we read 'Call of the Wild' for a book report."

She laughed. "I'll never forget it. You'd read out loud, and start crying, then I'd read and cry. It took us two days to do one chapter. I guess we're just a sentimental family."

"I was told once that our family 'wear our hearts on our sleeves'."

"Well, at least it shows we have hearts."

My heart swelled with pride as I looked into her beautiful blue eyes.

It took three days to remove the box full of staples. Though the nurses tried to be gentle, each one was, an experience. Then one by one the tubes were removed. I had a button that I could press to give me a shot of Demerol. At first it was great and I could rest when I needed. Soon I noticed I was continuously perspiring and itching. Sleep became impossible and nightmares plagued the nights. I asked if the medication could be at fault, and the doctor said no. After a week of growing discomfort, I asked the nurse to remove the automatic injector. She had to ask the doctor and he said no, reiterating that my discomfort could not be caused by the medication.

After two more days and nights of agony, I told the nurse I will pull it out myself. I was bluffing of course, but it worked and it was removed. Within two days the perspiring and itching stopped. As usual, I didn't get a chance to enjoy that victory before I had to face the next challenge.

Three nurses pushed a big green recliner chair into my room. "Doctor said time to get you sitting up."

Doctors' revenge for the injector, I thought.

They rolled me on my side and put my sling under me. It was over a month since I sat up. My mind frantically tried to anticipate everything that could go wrong and I issued a bunch of *requests*. I still had wires monitoring my heart, blood pressure, and the breathing tubes, which was my prime concern.

I pleaded to Marilyn. "Watch the ventilator connections." To one nurse, "please hold my head." A month of inactivity made my head unstable, and to everyone in general, "don't catch my dangling feet on the bed frame."

Sure enough the wires got tangled with the breathing tubes and I became disconnected from the ventilator. They opted to get me into the chair, then re-hook me, which was a logical thing to do, except I couldn't draw a breath. I shook my head frantically for attention and they saw I was turning blue. They stopped and reconnected me and life pumped back into my lungs. They untangled everything and sat me on the chair. Places I never knew existed throbbed with pain. They propped my weaving head with pillows and placed pillows between my feet and the cold hard floor. By the time they did everything, I said I had to get back to bed. The Max Sennet comedy repeated, except in reverse.

My heart sank deeper into depression.

"What kind of a clown have you become Ray?" It takes four people to get you into a chair."

I asked for a sedative before trying the chair again. It did help and my setting time slowly increased to half an hour.

Then came the biggest scare. The doctor told me I was ready to go home. Marilyn was briefed on the eight settings on my home ventilator, a Nebulizer (A mist machine to hook into my breathing tube to loosen phlegm in my lungs.), a suction machine, a trac cleaning kit and how to use them all. I listened to the bewildering mountain of things and shook my head in despair and fear.

"How in God's name can one girl handle all this?" I asked myself. "It takes four people to get me in and out of bed. It takes a hospital staff of intensive care nurses to answer my dozens of calls every night when my trac plugs with phlegm. How is Marilyn going to do all that?"

After the briefing, I posed my concerns to Marilyn.

"Ray, the only other choice is to put you in a nursing home until you get better, and *that*, is out of the question. Come hell or high water, we *will* get through this."

CHAPTER NINE

SUNSET

During the ambulance ride home, I was filled with apprehension. The chilling November rain was a harbinger of what was fast approaching. Marilyn and I sadly canceled our rented house in Florida. It would have been the second year on the Loxahatchie River. I sighed, picturing myself on the dock with my fishing pole. I half smiled as I remembered the day Mitzi ran full speed across the lawn and down onto the dock to bark at a passing Wave Runner. She couldn't stop and plunged into the choppy water. Marilyn had to pull her out. My warm thoughts were interrupted as the ambulance backed up to our garage door. The attendants wheeled me to my bedroom and lifted my ninety-eight pounds of bones onto the rented hospital bed. The room felt strange and empty without my old friend, the four-foot high rocking bed.

After some visitors left, I stared at the ceiling listening to the rhythm of my ventilator.

Whoosh, swish. Whoosh, swish. And the bubbling of the humidifier as it added moisture to my ventilator tube. Twice during the ride home and four times since being home Marilyn had to remove and clean my cannula. (The inner tube of my trac tube) My brother helped Marilyn get me up and into my chair for supper. He said to call when I was ready to go to bed. About ten o'clock I asked Marilyn to wheel me into the bedroom.

"Did you call Joe?" I asked.

"No. We'll do it ourselves."

"But Marilyn," I stammered. "A dozen things can go wrong."

Marilyn always trusted my judgment, and usually followed my suggestions, except when she set her mind to do something.

"Ray, we've got to do it sometime, and *now* is the hour."

When the chips are down, she is the one you'd want in your corner. The more crucial the decision, the stronger she becomes. She would make an excellent surgical nurse.

"Ready?" she asked.

"Yes," I answered, with my heart in my throat.

She hooked the Hoyer lift to the sling and pumped me up off the chair. She guided the tubes and swung me over the bed and slowly released the pressure in the lift. I gently settled onto the bed and she unhooked the chains. Deservedly proud of herself she said, "well, how was that?"

I motioned for her to set next to me. I pulled her head to my shoulder and whispered, "I love you more than you will ever know."

Marilyn hadn't slept a full night for over a month, so we arranged for a night nurse. While she got her first full night's sleep, the nurse cleaned my cannula thirty times.

Insurance covered the nurse for two weeks. I wanted to arranged to keep the nurse longer, but Marilyn insisted she would handle things herself.

Mitzi stayed on my bed day and night, only leaving long enough to eat and go outside to do her business. If anyone came into my room to shake hands or give me a greeting kiss, Mitzi would jump between us. My children learned no one could touch me without her jumping to protect me. So, being kids, they would tap me on my leg to watch her growl. She did the same to any size dog that came near me.

I puzzled over her complete devotion until I remembered the week I was home ill two years earlier. Mitzi was spay and under a year old. Some dogs want to be mothers so badly, they go into false pregnancy. (So the vet advised us when her breasts filled with milk.) She was miserable as she produced milk and couldn't get rid of it. I relieved her discomfort by gently squeezing her breasts to force the milk out. I continued the routine for a week until she finally dried up.

Her devotion wasn't to a master, but to her child. I firmly believe she became my mother that week, and I, her six-foot-six puppy. To be loved so completely was a wonderful feeling. She passed away at the age of fifteen. It has been sixteen years since she died, and I still tear thinking about her.

A month passed since I returned from the hospital. One evening Marilyn wheeled me to my desk in the living room.

With my elbows on the desk and my chin resting on my hands, my spirit sank. Fifty times a day and dozens of times a night Marilyn would rush to answer my ventilator alarm.

For the first time in forty years of conquering the impossible, my optimism began to fail me. I had performed miracles in the past inventing things and ways to prevail. I always looked forward to the eleven o'clock news *knowing* they would soon announce a way to rejuvenate dead nerves. But now, after thirty-five years, hope was fading. I called all over the United States but couldn't fine anyone in the same predicament. I was a dinosaur among dinosaurs. Very few doctors had encountered a Post Polio patient.

Despite my failing condition my wife made me feel like I was the sexiest man alive and *never* complained about her mountain of work.

Now, all I had to look forward to was killing her, inch by inch. She was working and worrying herself to death. That thought was unbearable. What a reward for being a Saint.

I killed my mother. I know I didn't ask for Polio, but that doesn't change the fact that I broke her wonderful spirit, and now I am doing it again.

My head sank deeper into my hands. My mind swirled into a frightening, hopeless abyss. I heard my mind proclaim.

"There is only one answer Ray, and you know what you have to do."

Marilyn had fallen asleep in the family room.

I opened my file drawer and lifted out my steel blue thirty-eight and a box of cartridges. I pulled back on the latch and the cylinder dropped open. I removed one cartridge from the box and slid it into the cylinder and closed it. I lined up the loaded chamber and pulled the hammer back.

I placed the barrel against my temple. I looked down at Mitzi asleep by my feet, as my tears formed a pattern on my trousers. I cautioned myself. "What if your hand slips as you pull the trigger, you better put the barrel in your mouth. Jesus Raymond! Do you always have to be so practical?"

I started to move the barrel from my temple when I suddenly remembered Nancy.

She worked for me when I was at the Plain Dealer, and her husband was a driver. They were married about a year when he was hit by a train. He lived, but suffered a broken spine and was confined to a wheelchair. After a year of treatment he returned to a desk job. A month later he put the muzzle of a forty-four magnum under his chin and blew his eye and part of his brains all over their bedroom ceiling. He lived for several weeks. Nancy and I would talk daily at work and I would try to console her. She eventually managed to accept his death, but she could not overcome the morbidness in their bedroom. The ceiling was cleaned and repainted, but she always saw the splattered blood stains.

The thought of what Marilyn would find stopped me. As I removed the bullet from the cylinder, I chastised myself. "I'm surprised at your selfishness Ray. To ease your pain you would cause her endless suffering every time she passed this room, and that you must not do. Bide your time until you can end your life accidentally and, elsewhere." I put the revolver back in the drawer as Marilyn walked in.

"Are you ready for bed?"

"Yes, I was just looking out the window daydreaming."

"I've been thinking, everyone enjoys your letters, and you are a good story teller. Why don't you write a book?"

"What kind of a book?"

"Everyone says you should write about your life."

"My life?" I chuckled. "Who would be interested in that?"

"I'm only repeating what others have said."

"I do have a story kicking around in my head. I would like to use the things I'd heard Dan talk about."

"The underworld?"

"Yes."

"Do you know enough about him to write a book?"

"Yes, and I'll tie it to the old West"

"Good. You can start tomorrow. I'm taking the dogs for a walk, then I'll put you to bed."

I looked out the window. The floodlight lit up the pond. The swirling snow created crazy patterns across the ice. I saw myself at the age of fourteen fishing in that same pond. When I tired of fishing I picked up my old 22 rifle and lay quietly until a snapping turtle would stick his head up. I aimed, not at a turtle, but at a Japanese soldier that was ready to hurt my brother. My little Remington became a heavy M-1 Garand Army rifle. I squeezed the trigger and I saved my brother again. I carried the big snapper a half mile to a friend that loved turtle soup.

My mind switched to a time my sister and I were shoveling snow off the pond. We built a shelter to keep us out of the wind while we put on our skates.

"Why not?" I thought. "Use your imagination to write. It will help to pass time."

The next day she bought some legal pads and I started writing. It did help keep my mind off the ventilator alarm.

"Just keep yourself sane until summer, then you know what you have to do."

I threw myself into writing the novel.

As England's heritage grew to prominence on the high seas, America's heritage is 'The Old West.' Only the strongest survived the brutal trip west. Bodies and graves of the weak and unlucky marked the long treacherous trails. Settlers faced weather, mountains, rivers, wild beasts, illnesses, Indians and cutthroats that would lay in wait for their next victim.

I was fortunate enough to make friends with a man that lived the second most colorful era in America, the 'Roaring Twenties.' He made and lost millions and knew personally most of the underworld characters. He won a boxcar full of money before he was finally ruled off the track at Hot Springs for fixing races. His stories were spellbinding. I wove his era, the stock market crash and the latter eighteen-hundreds together.

In two time periods I brought out government corruption, and the three-generation family that became entangled in the web of murder and intrigue.

I titled it, "Blood Trust."

I wrote and rewrote it several times by hand. Conversations with myself about my problems dwindled to a precious few. Before I started on my book, I would say a few words to the hall mirror as we passed it. The sight of the procession with Marilyn pushing my emaciated body in the antique wooden wheelchair became too painful, so I finally stopped looking. "You sure look like hell, Ray. No wonder your friends don't visit much. They hate for me to see their tears. Hold on, kid, just a few months to go."

When I would stop writing to rest my hand, I would look out the Pella windows at the forest creatures taking advantage of a winter thaw to drink from our spring fed pond. Over the weeks I witnessed the Winter reluctantly succumb to Spring.

Suddenly color was exploding with the warm May sun. The purple plums, apple and pear trees became full of beautiful blossoms.

That week I had my novel typed.

My best friend from high school stopped for a visit. "Hi Ray, you look good."

Without thinking I smiled and gave my usual pat answer. "Thanks, Bob. I do feel pretty good."

He sensed my matter-of-fact answer.

"No, I really mean it. You look altogether different."

Before I could answer, he continued. "I'm not kidding, you were really sad looking the last time I saw you."

After he left, I thought about his comments and asked Marilyn to wheel me to the mirror.

"By God!" I said out loud. "You *do* look better. A few months ago your face was hollowed and drawn. Now your cheeks are full, and I can't count your ribs."

Marilyn cut into my conversation. "I tied to tell you how much better you were looking."

"I thought you were just being kind. I haven't looked in the mirror for a long time."

"So how long are you going to set here and admire yourself?"

"As long as I keep feeling good about what I see." I smiled and laughed as I turned my head back and forth. "I'll be darned. I really do look better and come to think of it, I've been cleaning my own cannula, plus I can go without the ventilator for a half hour now."

Marilyn said. "Have you also noticed how long you sit in the chair? You're up from seven a.m. to eleven p.m. You only lay down for a couple hours in the afternoon."

My brain reeled with my wonderful new revelations.

"Push me back to my desk please. I have important plans to draw."

"Plans for what?"

"Fitting my ventilator and an extra battery on my old electric wheelchair."

I ordered three new batteries. Two to power the chair and one for my ventilator. I strapped my ventilator on top of the battery box behind my chair and had a box made to hold the breather battery, which was hung under the front part of my seat. A few weeks later Marilyn dropped me onto the power chair and ran the breathing tube to my trac. I buckled my seat belt and headed out our garage to the yard.

I delighted in the power and freedom the electric wheelchair gave me. I drove around my yard and into #1 greenhouse, down the aisle and stopped in the middle. The sun warmed me through the shade clothe and I reveled being out and with my friends again.

"Good morning, Mr.and Mrs. Hosta. Your colors are exceptionally beautiful. You must be eating well. And you, Royal Standard, I see your buds are starting to peep out of your home. I wonder, do you make your late entrance because you are Royalty?"

Mitzi was sitting in my lap looking at me. I rubbed her neck. "Are you happy to be, on the road again? I sure am. I know you've missed the miles we used to travel together, and now, thanks to the Boss upstairs, it looks like we will be good for another hundred thousand miles."

While I looked up, I glanced at Mitzi, and she was also looking up.

"You son-of-a-gun. You know who I'm talking to, don't you?"

I addressed another dozen plant varieties. I am usually extremely careful where I drive, but I was so excited with my first day out I spun my chair to leave and got tangled in the water hose. My chair was hopelessly stuck.

"Damn!" I exclaimed to Mitzi. "Why can't you pull the hose away?"

Her ears went back thinking I was scolding her.

"I know old girl, you would if you could. I hate to blow the boat horn and get the lecture."

I sounded the shrill horn, and my daughter and wife ran into the greenhouse.

"What's wrong?" they both yelled.

"Nothing, I just got tangled in the hose."

My daughter's face was flushed. "I thought the breather quit! You have to be more careful."

Marilyn, also out of breath chimed in. "How could you be so dumb? Don't you look where you're going?"

"Okay, Okay. Usually Mitzi watches, but she was too excited being on the road again. Tell you what. A short blast means no hurry. A long blast means, run like hell."

They untangled the hose and walked away mumbling.

"Present company excluded Mitzi, but sometimes women get overexcited."

As I drove out of the greenhouse, I smiled. "But, how lucky I am that they do."

Mitzi licked my hand.

"I see you agree old friend."

The hot sun felt wonderful. We stopped at the wooden deck I had built by the pond. The water level of the spring-fed pond was five feet lower than the ground around it. The deck was eight feet wide and extended over the water's edge. I decided to drive out to the end.

"It's been over a year since we could sit here and watch the mass of multicolored gold fish swim around the dock waiting to be fed."

My exuberance for the moment, and the year since I was out and around, caused me to relax my usual constant guard. My daughter called out from the kitchen window. "Want some bread to feed the fish?"

"Sure."

She sent her five-year-old son out. "Hi grandpa, here is the bread."

"Thanks Chad, go ahead and throw some in."

We watched as they went wild, leaping over each other for the crumbs. Then terror struck as I saw Chad's hand reaching for the control lever of my power chair, and before I could move or speak he grabbed the lever, as kids do, and pushed it. My chair lunged forward. My front wheels came inches from the edge. I was in the habit of shutting the power off when close to any drop offs, especially when children were around. They always found *that* lever and instinctively moved it. I had been run into tables, chairs and over toes until I got into the routine of shutting off the power. Not knowing what he was doing he automatically pulled it back. My chair stopped an inch from going over the edge and returned to my original spot. I quickly shut off the power and waited for my heart to get out of my throat. The picture of me going over the edge, flipping upside down with the three hundred pound chair landing on top of me nearly stopped my heart. It was fifteen minutes before I could speak.

"Mitzi, we almost bought it. First the hose, now one inch from sure death. I've got to remember to *never* relax, *never*. But, I guess that's part of the game I'm in." I looked up. "Boss, I appreciate being reminded about being vigilant, but I wish You'd be a little less dramatic. My heart can't stand too many like that."

A week later I was at my desk and Mitzi jumped up on the chair next to me.

"Yes, I'm right here. Don't worry. I wouldn't go outside without you."

I unlocked and opened my desk drawer for a pencil, and saw my revolver. "Mitzi, I almost did a stupid thing, didn't I? You know girl. I haven't felt this good in twenty years. I guess I really needed more air in my lungs. I've done a lot of thinking about something and now I have to tell Marilyn."

I called her. When she came into the office, I motioned for her to set next to, Mitzi.

"I made a decision. I think we should sell the house and business to one of the kids and build a summer house. Then we can spend the winters in Florida."

Marilyn jumped up knocking a startled Mitzi to the floor. "You're going to *what?*"

"This big house, yard and business is too much for you."

"My home! You're going to sell my home? *Never!*"

"Think, Marilyn. You're getting older and the constant work is going to kill you. If you run an engine wide open long enough, it will soon explode. You have been running wide open for more than thirty-five years."

"Where are you going to get the money to buy a lot, build a house and go to Florida?"

"That's my job to figure out, and I do have a plan."

"What plan?"

"I can split our lot and build across the pond."

"You'll never get that done, there isn't enough room. Then you have zoning, sewers, water and an easement to contend with." With a wry smile she finished. "What am I worried about? What you're saying is impossible."

As she left I turned to Mitzi. "We've been challenged."

Zoning required a minimum of 1300 square feet plus a two car attached garage, a major snag in my plans. I wanted to build a summer cottage with a car port. I looked through dozens of house plan books and couldn't find one to fit on my crazy shaped lot. The deep gorge on one side restricted all plans. The building area was 350 feet from the road and the sewer line. I knew I couldn't get enough fall at that distance. I was also short of the acreage needed for a septic tank.

So I drew my own plans, and the county allowed me to tap into the sewer trunk line that was only thirty-feet away. My brother witched and found an underground stream. I really lucked out with a helpful, caring builder. Clarence helped me smooth out the wrinkles, and the house would be started in the spring.

My wife was extremely unhappy. "You sold my home out from under me."

I told her I received last rights almost ten times. My body functions haven't been normal for forty years and I wanted her to have a house and yard that's easy to care for. Plus our daughter was next door for the time she will need help.

"You will always have a roof over your head and a fenced in yard for your dogs. (I hoped the dog part would help.) I know you only go to Florida for my health and hate to be away from your grandchildren." I stopped waiting for her response.

Tears streamed down her cheeks and she walked out of the room. "You're selling my house from under me."

All my talk was to no avail. The last thing I wanted to do was make her unhappy, but I felt strongly that it was the best for her. My doctor was amazed by my progress, but was apprehensive that we planned to go to Florida that winter, but I was determined.

We loaded two ventilators, a suction machine, an aspirator, two battery chargers, a nebulizer, a box of supplies, the Hoyer lift and two dogs. I had my van conversion company attach a holder for my Hoyer lift by the back seats. I calculated the measurements and angle so the lift would swing me from my chair to the left rear recliner seat. The van was overloaded requiring us to ship our clothes and medical supplies.

We were a team, and we started for Florida at five a.m. on a cold December morning. Marilyn said she would drive and handle everything. We had made the trip alone many times when I was still driving, but for her to do the driving, swing me into the back seat, prop and tie my legs, plug the ventilator in the cigarette lighter, get me back into my chair at the motel, then make a half dozen trips unloading everything, plus feed and walk the dogs, go for supper, take her shower, wash me and fall into bed. Then she could get up at three-thirty the next morning and start the whole process over, in reverse. So, I arranged for a friend to drive and help carry things in and out of the motel. Naturally she protested, but fell sound asleep within ten minutes after we were on the road.

That winter we bought a condo on the Intra Coastal in Jupiter, Florida. Then tragedy struck, my precious Mitzi became ill. The vet found she was full of tumors and her vital organs were shutting down. She had to be put to sleep. Our hearts were broken. My brave wife held her in her arms when the vet injected her. I had to remove all her pictures because I would break down every time I looked at my beautiful, second mother, Mitzi.

We returned to Ohio May first. That summer we bought a Manchester Terrier and named her Tiger. It took several years before I could display the pictures of my Mitzi.

50 YEARS OF MIRACLES

We sold our house and business to my daughter and son-in-law. We lived with them while the house was being built next door. As Marilyn became involved picking appliances, carpeting and tile, she soon forgot her old house was sold.

My mind had pictured the finished product. The long driveway along the pond was picturesque. I designed the kitchen to get the morning sun and she could watch the geese and ducks on our pond from the window over her sink. The glass doors in the great room opened onto a deck overlooking a wooded gorge.

As much as I loved Ohio in the summer, I hated it in the winter. Before Polio I enjoyed the seasons. But now my body reacted violently to cold plus winter confined me indoors.

We left for Florida in November and my health and stamina continued to improve. For three years the best of two worlds was enjoyed.

But as usual, when things are going good and I feel 'normal,' I'm reminded of how precarious life is for me.

One glorious morning in July, I sat on the deck eating breakfast. Our spring-fed pond was down a foot. The Chinese White Amor (algae eating fish) had ballooned to football girth. Their yard long bodies dwarfed the big bass and rainbow colored goldfish. I had my usual morning talk to nature.

"Good morning sun, thank you for your warmth of body, and you, Red Birds, for your soul filling melodies, and you lush trees with your new leaves that produce the sweet fresh smell of spring. My heart swells with what I see. The grass giving its morning dew to the thirsty, busy bees. The chipmunks flying from branch to branch, and I hear the verse. Mine eyes have seen the glory." I finished breakfast and spent the morning at Deb's checking things at the nursery. At noon I drove my power chair around the pond to my house, up the ramp and onto the deck. Marilyn had lunch ready and my friend John and

193

I played our daily card game, Crazy Eights. He worked at the nursery for over a dozen years and was part of our family. After lunch Marilyn said she had to go shopping. She laid me down, connected me to the breather on my headboard and covered me. As she put the Q-tip box on my lap, she told me she had the beeper. I had the beeper number on a piece of paper in the Q-tip box.

My daughter was next door if an emergency arose. I drifted off to sleep. The alarm went off on my breathing machine waking me. The ventilator quit working for some reason. I reached up and tried tapping it, but it did not respond.

"Don't worry Ray," I assured myself. "Call Debbie and she will be over in a minute. You've gone a half hour on your own before."

I picked up the phone next to my pillow, punched in her number and put the receiver next to my ear. Nothing! I tapped the phone, still nothing. The plug was in the phone, but still no dial tone. Panic struck my heart as if it were stabbed by an icicle.

"Relax Ray, use the air horn."

I kept it on my headboard in case Marilyn was vacuuming or washing and could not hear my bell. I blasted it over and over hoping Debbie would hear it, but she did not.

"What are you going to do Ray? Marilyn could be gone a couple hours."

That thought increased my fear. I felt constriction and pain in my chest and it was only five minutes since the machine shut off.

"Ray," I ordered myself. "Keep calm. Relax, and breath slowly. You'll be all right, Debbie's kids are always running in and out of the house."

I tried to concentrate on a television program which worked for a few minutes, then I felt myself begin to tremble.

"RAY! STOP IT! Think of something to take your mind off of the clock."

But my eyes were drawn back to it. It was more than ten minutes since the ventilator shut off. I began to picture Marilyn returning home and finding me dead, or worse, comatose. Then if I could be revived, I'd be brain dead from lack of oxygen.

"Stop that shit!" I ordered myself. I had some weak abdominal muscles that would expand my stomach taking air into my lungs then I would relax and gravity would push the air out. My machine gave me nineteen breaths a minute, so I watched the clock and tried to get by on fifteen to conserve my weak muscles.

Twenty minutes passed and I couldn't stop trembling, anticipating my muscles would just quit. I felt myself struggling to maintain the fifteen breaths per minute, so I cut them to ten.

Twenty-five minutes passed and I felt myself perspiring. I grabbed the phone again and pounded it against the headboard but still no dial tone. I felt my stomach muscles quiver trying to maintain their job to keep me alive. They were reaching the point of exhaustion and I knew it.

Again I pictured Marilyn finding me dead, and worse, blaming herself.

"Oh God, is this how it's going to end? All these years she has struggled to keep me alive and to lose me because of a telephone malfunction."

The clock showed thirty-five minutes had passed. I had to do something, but what? "If you were sitting up, your stomach would hang out and you could squeeze the air out with your arms. Hey dummie, run the head of the bed up and try that."

I pushed the button on my control and the bed sat me up. My stomach expanded. I held my left pelvic bone with my right hand and my right pelvic bone with my left and squeezed the air out. I relaxed my arms and my stomach dropped sucking air into my lungs.

It was working! But after five minutes, my left arm wore out and my right was tiring fast. I lowered the bed and my rested stomach muscles did their task while my arms rested. Each time I switched, my endurance lessened. I looked at the clock, fifty-eight minutes. My arms and stomach muscles were aching. Each time I ran the bed up and down, I wondered if it would be the last time.

Then I heard the dogs bark, Marilyn was home, but she was still outside.

"Oh God," I thought. "Will she go next door to Debbie's before she comes in?"

I quickly grabbed the air horn hoping there was enough compressed air left for another blast. There was, and thank God she heard it and ran in. She recycled the machine and it started pumping air to my starving lungs. How wonderful it tasted. The air felt like cool spring water to a parched throat. She found the vacuum cleaner had knocked the phone connection out of the wall. I lamented, thinking that once again, I have ripped another piece out of her heart.

Since then, I always check the phone before she leaves, plus I now keep a cellular phone with me.

One evening a few weeks later the eleven o'clock news was about to start when I turned the T.V. off and headed for my bedroom. As I rode past Marilyn's bedroom, I looked in. Her glasses were on her forehead and the book in her hands had slipped onto her bed cover. She was asleep in the same position I saw her two hours earlier. Molly was asleep next to her with her four paws sticking straight up in the air.

"Poor kid," I thought. "You never get much read before you're out. Now I have to wake you up to throw my carcass into bed. What a routine I have stuck you with. Every night, every morning and every afternoon since the accident in '79. Before that I could get in and out of bed myself. But since then—."

I hung my head in despair for her. I looked at her face that was once smooth and young.

"Mare, how many lines I've given you. How many aching overworked joints and muscles you have because of me. Those legs that were so long and beautiful now show the miles they have carried you *and* me. What have I done to you? Since 1979, eighteen years. My God, Raymond, for eighteen years she has performed the same routine of getting you in and out of bed twice a day. Three hundred and sixty five days a year times eighteen years equals six thousand five hundred and seventy days, times four, WOW!"

"Almost twenty five thousand times!"

I shook my head in amazement as the figures sunk in. I tapped on her door then drove my power chair into my bathroom. I sat dumbfounded in front of the mirror.

"Twenty-five thousand times getting you in and out of bed. Good God Almighty."

She yelled in from her bedroom. "You ready?"

"Yes," I answered. I removed my trac tube and cleaned it with hot water, unbuttoned my shirt, unhooked my corset and drove by the bed. She came into my room and removed my shirt, corset, shoes and pants. I drove under the Hoyer lift and she attached the four hooks to the sling. She pushed the button and my body lifted off the seat.

"At least the power lift is better than the old pump one." I said, trying to inject a positive thought. She nodded, still half asleep.

"You are amazing, girl. Do you know how many times you have put me in and out of bed? Six thousand five hundred and seventy days at four lifts a day equals about twenty-five thousand times."

I waited for her response. She pushed the lift over the bed and dropped me onto the mattress and answered casually, "well, someone has to do it."

She rolled me on one side and tucked the sling under, then rolled me the other way and removed it. She covered me, put Q-tips on my lap, hooked me up to my second ventilator, knelt on the floor and plugged one charger to my breather battery and the second charger to my wheelchair batteries.

She kissed me goodnight and said. "That's twenty-five thousand and one."

I smiled as she set the timer on my TV, and left to let the dogs out for the last time.

"What a girl," I said to myself. "She never gave it a thought. Six-thousand, five-hundred and seventy days without missing a day, and without a complaint.

My trac started to whistle from a plug of phlegm. I removed my inner-cannula, then cleaned it with a Q-tip.

"Well," I said to myself. "That's one. Another dozen times and you'll be able to go to sleep. Boy, would it be nice to lie down and go to sleep without these cleaning's. I wonder how many people give a thought to how lucky they are to go to bed, and right to sleep."

As I cleaned it the second time, I consoled myself. "At least you can clean it yourself. I bet Christopher Reeves would like to have enough hand movement to clean, his own trac. Moreover, you don't have to ring for Mare like you did at first.

"How did she survive that first year after the operations, having to get up a dozen times a night?"

As I said my prayers, I told Him, "thanks Boss, for what I have. I don't deserve special treatment over the thousands like Chris, but please take care of Marilyn. She asks for nothing and gives every ounce of herself every day.

A slight setback in December. I had a gall bladder attack.

Because of muscle loss from Polio, the doctors couldn't do Laparoscopic surgery. I got the old fashioned fifteen inch scar. Again, the hospital allowed Marilyn stay with me day and night.

We were eleven hundred miles from family. They offered to fly down, but our new friends in our complex came to our rescue. They walked and fed our dogs and gave Marilyn the support she needed. I will be eternally grateful to them all.

A few days after we got home from the hospital, Marilyn suggested I go outside and let the sun help heal my incision. The sun felt great as I watched the action on the Intra Coastal. I have visited Florida a dozen times since 1955 and there was always something spellbinding about Florida that's been missing the last three years. Jupiter is a great town. Besides being home to Perry Como, Burt Reynolds, golf greats Arnie Palmer, Greg Norman and Fred Couples it has another distinction. It's closeness to the powerful twenty-mile wide Gulf Stream. Along the East coast of the United States the Gulf Stream is thirty miles offshore. In Jupiter, it starts three miles out which creates a breeze and moderate weather. Being on a ventilator, air is pumped into my lungs through a tracheotomy tube in my throat. All air bypasses my nose. Marilyn was walking our pets and the connection in the tube from the ventilator disconnected. I didn't panic because my mobile phone was a minute from Marilyn's beeper and I could breathe for at least fifteen minutes. While I looked for the separation, I began drawing air through my nose and like a miracle, I found my old, wonderful Florida.

I realized then that I was missing God's wonderful conglomerate of nature's aromas.

Those few breaths through my nasal passages electrified nerves to my brain, opening stored memories from my past. The salt air mixing with the pungent hibiscus and Oleanders combined to remind me of pleasant times from yesteryear. With a finger on the tube in my throat I drew more air through my nose forcing other glorious memories to stir my soul. I was suddenly with my mother and grandmother in Ft. Lauderdale in a backyard cookout. Though that was forty-two years earlier, I was there.

The next breath, and I was under a huge Pine tree in my friend

Ron's yard in Pompano. We were drinking beer, laughing and solving the world's problems.

Though they have all been dead for decades, the memories were most refreshing. Then the odor of oil rich gas from the boats returned me to my honeymoon and the glass bottom boat at Winter Gardens. Then my lungs reminded me it was time for air and I reconnected the ventilator tube. My wonderful excursion down memory lane was over. Although the forty-pound ventilator keeps me alive, I do resent the years it deprived me of those priceless trips. The multitude of nature's aromas are all over the world, spiced by local smells and blended by God's warm sun. At my grandmother's house on Sundays, ambrosia poured from her kitchen. Cooking meat, cabbage and spices wove into the very fabric of her lace-covered couch and chairs. The wooden floor and heavy wallpaper carried the smell of fresh baked bread and Hungarian pastry. My mouth watered remembering those smells from sixty years earlier. God lets us store the smells of our lifetime and occasionally we are reminded of wonderful times past. One day my five-year-old grandson had commented. "That woman smells like church." His storehouse is filling.

Marilyn returned. "I think you've had enough sun for the first day."

"But not enough smells."

"Smells, what are you talking about?"

"Just something between me and my nose."

"I think you've been in the sun too long. Are we going to the clubhouse Friday night?"

"Sure, why do you ask?"

"I have to decide on a dish to take."

"No problem, I'll be your dish."

"Come on, let's go for a ride. You need to cool off."

"Okay, where?"

"Let's get a sandwich and go to the inlet and watch the surfers."

We got a couple burgers and parked on the edge of the beach. The ocean was its usual shades of beautiful blues. Every time I look at it, I thank God for my eyesight. There were a couple dozen young surfers waiting for 'the Big One'. There were tables for picnickers and the beach was full of sun worshipers. Children were building sand castles while their parents watched. It was a peaceful sight.

Then I said. "Show off!"

Looking toward the surfers, she asked. "Who?"

"That old geezer with the walker."

"You mean that white haired man with his wife?"

"Yeah, him."

"What do you mean showoff? He can hardly walk."

"He's not only a showoff, but I bet he complains about having to use a walker."

"Okay, what's your point?"

"I'd like to go up to him and say, you're a lucky old fart."

"Ray!"

"No, I'm serious. He is lucky, and I wonder if he realizes it?"

"He'd probably ask if you escaped from some happy house."

"Then I'd tell him. You've spent a lifetime being normal. Unlimited from going wherever you wanted, and you could play ball and swim with your grandchildren, and now you're here in Florida growing old, with dignity. You may not think so, but here you are walking on the beach with your woman. If you have to go to the john right now, you can. Think of all the things you can do *independently*, count your blessings."

"That's a good speech Ray. Go tell him."

"Are you nuts?" I laughed. "I might hurt his feelings."

"Or maybe he might think of your words and feel better."

"Me thinks, my dear, we have grasped each other's soul."

Printed in the United States
59017LVS00002B/67-84

9 781424 128754